100 cosy projects

100 cosy projects
for a comfortable home

MQP

DESIGN BY Balley Design Associates

Published by MQ Publications Limited
12 The Ivories, 6–8 Northampton Street, London N1 2HY
Tel: +44 (0)20 7359 2244   Fax: +44 (0)20 7359 1616
e-mail: mail@mqpublications.com
website: www.mqpublications.com

ISBN: 0 84072 353 X

Printed and bound in England

1 3 5 7 9 10 8 6 4 2

introduction	6
window dressing	12
furniture	34
linens	54
storage	80
lighting	106
display	124
entertaining	152
christmas	172
outdoor living	198
templates	230
index	253

contents

introduction

More than ever the home has become our sanctuary. It is the place to which we can retreat and devote time to ourselves—our recreation and recuperation. In order to find the peace and reassurance we so desperately need at the beginning of the twenty-first century, it is essential that this place be an expression of who we are and, indeed, who we have been. Given the choice, most of us would not want to throw out everything we have and give our homes a complete makeover, because home style is essentially built up layer upon layer, year after year. It tells the story of our lives, from family hand-me-downs to objects that have treasured memories attached from a vacation or particular shopping expedition.

And the overall decor has to be able to draw together these disparate elements into a whole to create a restful environment. By following a few standard guidelines, you cannot go wrong. Choose simple shapes and clean lines for furniture; many patterns become dated, so opt for classic patterns such as checks and stripes; use color to unify items or alter proportions by creating optical illusions. Rather than pick out architectural details, which can look "busy," paint walls in a uniform color or use a similar shade on baseboards (skirting-boards), dados, and picture rails. This provides a serene backdrop against which to arrange furniture and hang a stunning piece of artwork. Continue to work with the existing architecture for curtains. Where possible, fit them within the window recess so that you can see the architrave. Otherwise fit a curtain pole and finials that extend a good way on either side of the window so that the curtains do not mask the window when they are

drawn. The home also has to be a place you can manage to live in with ease, where children can play, pets can roam, and friends can relax. It has to be low maintenance, with removable, washable covers and easy-to-clean surfaces. This is where natural materials prove so successful, because they have a timeless quality to them and age beautifully. Plain sanded and sealed floorboards, stone floors, and natural undyed grasses such as sisal and coir are hard-wearing and look good. Their neutral colors also enable them to blend with whatever color scheme you have chosen for the furnishings in the room. Utility fabrics such as cotton duck, denim, and linen sheeting are all natural fibers that age well and withstand the rigors of washing, so they are ideal for curtains, bedding, and cushion covers. Add in soft wools and extravagant silks for more luxurious items.

The garden, too, is an extension of our living space and contributes so much to our sense of well-being. During the summer months, our time at home can be transplanted outside—covered director's chairs grouped around a table for drinks on the patio, a hammock strung between two branches for reading or listening to music, and even for the less-enthusiastic gardener, planting a window box or hanging basket. Perhaps here, more so than inside, you can allow yourself to go crazy with color, choosing hot pinks and oranges to mimic the shades of summer.

So the comfortable home is intensely personal. It evolves over time, the layout shifting to accommodate your lifestyle, with new items being added on a regular basis. As a space that you create yourself, it makes sense to design

and make your own soft furnishings and accessories, and customize existing or new furniture and storage items. By taking the personal approach, the possibilities become endless. Rather than finding yourself trapped in the limited color range on offer for furnishings in the department stores, you can choose from a vast selection of colors and fabrics. There is a great satisfaction to be found in visiting craft and home improvement stores to find exactly the right color and bead combination for a table runner, or seeking out the suppliers for a particular fabric you have set your heart on. All these things are therapeutic, giving us a sense of control over our environment and the ability to effect change should we want to.

With this in mind, the projects in this book are designed to provide inspiration, to set the reader off along new avenues of creativity. They all meet the criteria of simplicity of design and construction, balance between function and style, good availability of materials, and ease of maintenance. They favor discreet detailing over fancy trimmings—simple eyelet headings and buttoned tabs for curtains, and ties and buttons for cushions. Often elegant stitching is enough—a couple of rows of topstitching around the edges of cushions and other linens, or blanket stitching to hold together the layers of a set of place mats. Materials are chosen to suit the projects—hard-wearing fabrics for outdoor furniture such as garden chairs and hammocks, sturdy cardboard for storage bins and shoe boxes. The beauty of many of the projects lies in the use of unusual materials, such as handmade paper for a blind, knitted hemp with glass beads caught into the design for a curtain, and corrugated cardboard for a magazine rack.

Getting lost in the planning and execution of a particular project can provide physical and emotional respite from the stresses of everyday life, and you can enjoy the fruits of your labors for many years to come. Above all, choose colors and materials that lift your spirit, and do not feel bound by the materials suggested within these pages.

before you start

The projects in this book do not require special skills, but if you are new to a particular technique, such as stenciling, it is always good to practice first. Apart from the curtains and cushions, which need a sewing machine, the majority of the sewing projects can be done by hand. A basic sewing kit, which includes dressmaker's scissors, dressmaker's chalk, a tape measure, pins, sewing needles, and basting cotton, is essential. Any sewing equipment that does not fall into this basic kit is noted in the materials list. Many of the tools that are listed can be found in an average household tool kit—sandpaper, hammer, nails, pliers, etc. Other items, such as pens, pencils, ruler, metal measuring tape, hole punch, etc., are common household items.

Always be aware of your personal safety. Keep a good supply of blades for your craft knife. Blades become blunt quite quickly, producing a torn, ragged edge, and are then dangerous because of the extra effort required. Always work in a well-ventilated space when using powerful glues. For mosaic work, you must protect your eyes and hands at all times from flying shards of tile. When breaking tiles, place the tiles or glass in a strong sack and take this outside before smashing them with a hammer, and always wear goggles. When cutting tiles and wire, wear goggles and rubber gloves. Always read through the instructions carefully and make sure you have all the materials on hand before starting any project, and test on scraps, if necessary.

stenciling and stamping While stamps and stencils can be purchased, you will sometimes need to make your own. For stenciling, trace or photocopy the design and tape it to a cutting mat. Secure your stencil material over the top. This can be stencil film or cardboard, or a clear piece of acetate. Holding a craft knife with the blade away from you, cut through the film along the lines.

When stenciling, pour a little paint onto a plate, dip in the tip of a dry stencil brush, and blot off the excess on a cloth or paper towel. Hold the brush perpendicular to the surface, and working away from the edges toward the center, apply the paint, building up the color gradually. Stippling, dabbing, flicking, or rotating the brush each gives a different result. If the paint bleeds under the edge of the stencil, you have used too much. It is vital that you clean your stencils frequently, especially when they are reversed to achieve the inverse of the design. Alternatively, you could cut extra stencils.

Stamps are cut from foam or rubber, which can then be glued to a block of wood for easy handling. Wood allows even pressure to be applied. High-density (condensed) rubber foam is good for detailed designs. Trace the designs off the source using tracing paper and use spray adhesive to attach the tracing to the foam. Cut this out using a craft knife. Use a small roller or a brush to apply paint to the stamp, then press the stamp firmly onto the surface. Do not use too much paint, as it will spoil the design.

wirework Two of the wirework projects—the aluminum mesh basket and the egg basket—are made from twisted wire, which you will have to make yourself. Twisting strands of wire together has many advantages. It looks decorative, it adds strength, and it increases flexibility, making it easier to create smooth spirals and curves. It is easy to twist strands of soft or fine wire, such as copper, together using a handheld drill. This method makes it possible to twist wire evenly and as loosely or tightly as needed. Cut a length approximately half a length longer than the required twisted length. Bend it around a stair baluster and feed the cut ends into the chuck of a hand drill. Tighten to secure the ends. Keep the wire taut and turn the drill. When you have twisted the wire to the required tension, undo the chuck to release. Cut the other end from the baluster with wire cutters.

Hard or thicker wire, such as galvanized or green gardening wire, is better twisted by hand using a wooden spoon. Cut a length about three times longer than the required twisted length. Bend the wire in half around a baluster and join the two ends by twisting them together in a counterclockwise direction. Hold the handle end of the spoon in one hand and the bowl end in the other. Twist the wire in a clockwise direction. Pull the wire taut and keep it horizontal for an even twist. When the wire is twisted to your satisfaction, transfer your hold from the spoon to the wire and allow the spoon to unwind slightly and release the tension of the wire. Cut the wire free.

To make coils, which are used as a decorative and structural feature in traditional wirework, wrap the wire tightly around a wooden spoon handle or dowel, depending on the size of the coil needed. Remove the coil from the wood. To flatten, if necessary, carefully and evenly flatten each loop by pressing each one tightly between your fingers. Stretch the coil so that the individual loops are separate, then allow them to overlap.

A relaxed home is dressed in curtains and blinds that have a casual elegance, created through the use of simple designs, clean lines, and understated decorations. Dispense with elaborate swags and gathers, and opt instead for a single width of fabric that lends itself to a more tailored treatment. Hang the finished curtain with loops and ties, hooks, shackles, or clips, so that when drawn, the curtain hangs straight to highlight the quality of the material and

the pattern in the weave. Choose fabrics that complement the mood—informal denim and well-laundered linen sheets and tablecloths to frame a window, breezy organza and translucent handmade papers to soften the light, or a collection of shimmering beads to form a screen. Keep patterns simple with classic stripes and checks that can be used to emphasize or disguise dimensions.

window dressing

glorious organza

Floaty and feminine, organza hangs beautifully without relying on gathers. You can be brave with color, because the light can pour through, keeping the tones subtle. The lightweight organza is offset with robust flat-fell seams and double topstitching and finished off with exquisite shell buttons.

materials

Silk organza in two colors (see measuring up)
Sewing thread in the main/strongest color
Shell buttons
Sewing machine
Sewing kit

measuring up

This single curtain is fitted to the outside of the architrave. Measure the full width of the architrave and add 8 in. to allow for two finials and another 2½ in. per panel. Divide the width of the curtain by your chosen number of panels to determine how wide each panel will be. (An odd number of panels will look better and you can have the main color on both outside edges. If the figure does not divide neatly, make the curtain slightly wider.) The length is from the curtain rail to the floor or windowsill as preferred, plus 4 in. for turnings. Allow extra material for tabs. Double-check your calculations.

1 Cut out the panels from the two lengths of organza, allowing a 1 in. seam allowance along both sides of each panel. **2** Cut one tab for each panel plus one extra, measuring 2 x 6 in. Fold the tabs in half lengthwise, right sides together. Stitch across one short seam and along the long raw edges. Trim the seams and turn right side out. Position the long seam at one side. Press. **3** Arrange the panels on a flat surface in alternating colors. Pin, then stitch together using flat-fell seams (see step picture). **4** Turn in the raw edge of each tab. Pin this end to the wrong side of the curtain top with one to the top of each seam joining the panels. Baste. **5** Taking in the tabs as you go, use a sewing machine to sew a double hem all around the curtain, making a double line of topstitching. **6** Bring the loose end of the tab to the front. Center a button on the tab and sew it on through all thicknesses.

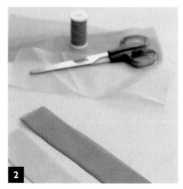
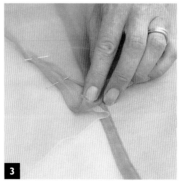
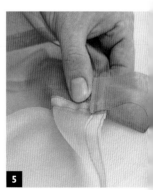

unstructured blind

This delightfully casual window treatment is made from an old French linen sheet, adapted with just two box pleats at the top to fit the width of the window. It is drawn up by three cords threaded through rows of rings at the back, which let the linen fall into its natural voluptuous folds.

materials

Linen (see measuring up)
Sewing thread to match
Wooden batten 2 x 1 in., cut to the
width of the architrave
Calico to cover the batten
Small brass rings, enough for three
vertical rows with rings
spaced 10 in. apart
Safety pins, in equal number to the
brass rings
Four large screw eyes
Nonstretch cord, three times the
sum of the length plus three times
the width of the blind
Staple gun or upholstery tacks
Blind pull
Angle irons
Cleat
Sewing machine
Sewing kit

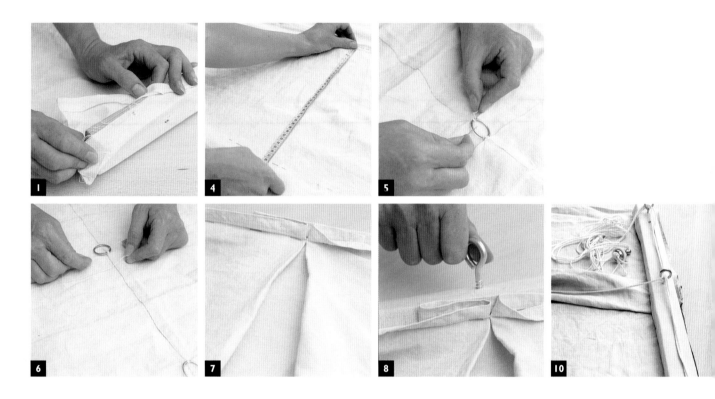

measuring up

This treatment is designed to hang inside the window reveal. Measure the width and length of the window. Add an extra 6 in. to the length and 2 in. to the width for turnings. This is the absolute minimum requirement for the fabric. If you have a piece that is larger, so much the better. The maximum length is about one-and-a-half times the length of the window.

1 Cut a piece of calico sufficient to cover the batten, allowing extra fabric for turnings. Turn in the raw edges, wrap around the batten, and staple into position along one narrow edge. **2** Turn in any raw edges on the linen and sew or machine stitch. **3** Ensure that any features, such as the monogram, are centered close to the bottom edge where they will be seen and place the blind right side down on a flat surface. **4** Down the length of the fabric, measure and mark the center line using pins. Measure and mark a line down the halfway point between the center and left-hand edge. Repeat for the right-hand edge. **5** Sew a brass ring close to the bottom edge of the fabric at each of the three marked lines. **6** On each line, measure 10 in. up from the first ring and stitch on another. Repeat every 10 in. up the length, but space the last ring 16 in. from the previous one. You may want to try out the positions with safety pins

first to make sure you are happy with the finished look before you start sewing on the rings. **7** Staple the top edge of the blind to a 1 in. edge of batten. If the fabric is too wide, make box pleats at intervals to fit. The stapled edge fits to the wall. **8** Fix three screw eyes to the 2 in. wide underside of the batten in line with the three rows of rings. **9** Fix the remaining screw eye at one end of the batten through which all the cords will be threaded. **10** Cut the cord into three equal lengths. Tie one end to each of the bottom three rings. Thread the cord up through the rings, along the batten, through the screw eyes, and to the screw eye at the end of the blind. Gather the lengths together and thread them through the blind pull. Trim the cords to equal lengths and make a knot at the bottom. **11** Fix the batten to the wall using the angle irons. Screw the cleat to the window frame on the same side as the extra screw eye. Pull up the blind and secure the cords in the cleat.

leaf blind

This blind gives the appearance of leaves falling outside the window. The paper used is a strong type of abaca tissue. Two layers are sandwiched together with spray adhesive, trapping the stylized cut leaves between them. Hang the blind using curtain clips or stitch it onto a decorative pole.

materials

Two sheets of abaca tissue paper
Orange and green handmade plant
or flower papers
Paper string
Curtain rod to fit the window and
screw eyes
Craft knife and cutting mat
Spray adhesive
Glue stick
Needle
Pencil
Drill

1 Trace the leaf templates on page 230 and use them to draw about twenty different shapes on the handmade papers. **2** On the cutting mat, cut around the outline with the craft knife and then carefully cut out and remove all the small triangles representing the veins of each leaf. **3** Cut the two abaca tissue sheets 1 in. larger all around than the window. Leaving a border of at least 2 in. around the edge, arrange the leaves on one sheet of the tissue paper until you have a pleasing and balanced pattern. **4** Fix the leaf shapes in position with spray adhesive. **5** Spray the entire sheet of abaca tissue with adhesive. Match the bottom corners of the second sheet of abaca tissue and smooth the paper toward the top with the flat of your hand. **6** Press under a ½ in. double hem around the four sides. Miter each corner for a neat finish. Glue the hem in place with the glue stick. **7** Drill holes into the ends of the curtain rod and screw in the screw eyes. Measure and mark the position for the curtain rod on the window frame. Drill holes in alignment with the screw eyes and screw the hooks in place in the window frame. Hang the blind by making loops of paper string through the top with a needle and slipping it onto the curtain rod.

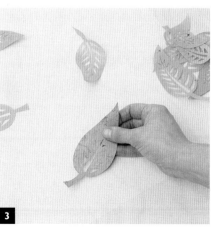
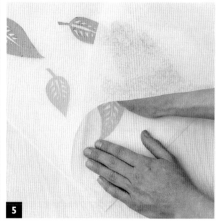

shackled heading

These full-length curtains, made from heavy woven cotton, are hung on a sleek, polished, steel curtain pole with French yachting shackles fed through an eyelet heading. The eyelets are carefully placed so that they always fall on a cream stripe, giving the curtains a tailored look.

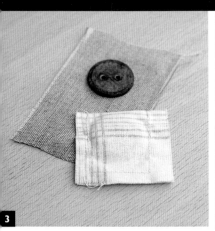

3

4

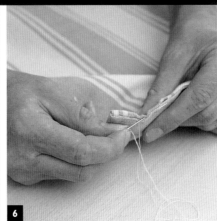

6

7

materials

Heavy curtain fabric (see measuring up)
Linen/cotton union fabric for lining (see measuring up)
Sewing thread to match
Lightweight fabric scraps
Eyelets (internal diameter ½ in.); allow at least one per 8 in. of the width, and assembly tool
One yachting shackle for each eyelet
Four curtain weights
Hammer
Sewing machine
Sewing kit

measuring up

These curtains are fitted to the outside of the architrave. For a pair of curtains, measure the full width of the architrave and add 8 in. to allow for two finials plus 4 in. for seam allowances. Halve this final figure to determine the width you need to cut for each curtain. The length is from the curtain rail to the floor or the windowsill as preferred, plus 4 in. for turnings. Double-check your measurements.

1 Cut two curtains in the main fabric and two linings to your measurements. **2** From scraps, cut eight squares to make four pockets large enough for the weights. **3** To make the pockets, place two squares right sides together. Stitch three sides, place the weight inside, and slipstitch to close. **4** Place one curtain on a flat surface, right side up. Place a lining right side down on top. Pin together. Start at the top of one long edge and stitch down the length, across the width at the bottom, and up the second length. **5** Trim the seams and press open. Snip off the corners. Stitch one weight to the lining at each bottom corner. **6** Turn the curtain right side out. Turn in the top raw edges and slipstitch to close. Press. **7** Mark the positions for the eyelets and fix them in place using the assembly tool and a hammer. Place a shackle through each eyelet. Repeat for the second curtain.

beaded screen

The joy of this room screen is that rather than closing off two spaces, it visually divides them. As the light hits the screen, the soft-edged beads play with the light without dazzling. The lime-wash effect on the frame gives the screen a soft, natural look that freshens up the natural color of the twine.

materials

1½ in. thick square oak panels
Four 3 in. brass hinges
One large roll of garden twine (or string of your choice)
465 crystal oval glass beads, 1 x ¾ in.
300 crystal disk glass beads, ¾ in.
Ninety-six crystal disk glass beads, 1 x ¼ in.
Approximately 2 oz. of candle wax
White emulsion paint
2 in. paintbrush
All-purpose clear adhesive
Clear wood sealer
Newspaper
Drill and wood drill bits
Small, round wood file
Old can and saucepan
Old plastic container in which to dilute the paint
Measuring tape
Pencil
Scissors
Medium-grade sandpaper
Sponge

1 Have a carpenter make the screen for you, using the following dimensions. The screen has three panels; each has two lengths 64 in. tall, and two 18 in. across the width, one at the top and one 3 in. from the bottom. It is important to use a hardwood so that the frame does not warp. **2** Work on one panel at a time. Along the inside top and bottom of each frame, mark fourteen points (or any even number of your choice) with a pencil 1 in. apart. **3** Using a drill bit closest to the correct size for your gauge of twine, drill holes from the inside out on the frame. Run the wood file into the holes to clear them. Use the sandpaper to clean the edges of the holes and all relevant surfaces. **4** To get a "limed" effect on the frame, add 2 tablespoons of emulsion to 14 fl. oz. of water and mix well. Soak a sponge, wring it out until just damp, and rub it all over the frame once, then go back, layering the paint to reach the density that you prefer. If some areas get too dense, wipe them down with a clean, wet sponge to remove some of the paint. **5** Leave to dry, then apply a thin coat of the clear wood sealer and leave to dry for twenty-four hours. **6** Measure the height of the frame from floor to top and multiply by three. Cut lengths of twine to this measurement for half the total number of holes across the top of the frame. (For forty two holes, you need to cut twenty-one lengths.) **7** Put the candle wax into a can and place inside a saucepan with enough water to cover the bottom. Gently heat the saucepan to melt the wax, then carefully remove the tin. **8** Dip the ends of the twine into the wax by up to 4 in. to coat them, keeping the wax application thin. Lay them out straight on some old newspaper to harden. This will make it easier to pass the twine through the beads and the holes in the framework. **9** Take a length of twine and run it up through the first hole in the top of one of the panels and back down through the next hole, keeping the two hanging halves equal. Repeat for the remaining holes across the frame. **10** Follow the chart on page 230 for the beading sequence and measurements. Use one or two overhand knots under each bead to hold it in place. **11** Start beading across the rows from the top, then down row by row, measuring the distances between the beads to keep them even. **12** When you reach the bottom of each panel, push the waxed ends of twine through the drilled holes in the bottom of the frame. **13** Leave for a couple of days to allow the twine to stretch with the weight of the beads: You may need to readjust the beads at the bottom. **14** To finish the screen, tie off the twine in pairs on the underside of the bottom of the frame, double-knotting each pair. Don't pull the twine too taut, but make sure that the knot is tight. **15** Apply a small amount of clear adhesive to each knot and leave to dry. Cut off the excess twine close to the knots.

denim curtain

Faithful to the particularities of jeans, this curtain features double line topstitching and metal rivet buttons. This no-fuss fabric demands a no-fuss fixing—any wooden pole will suffice. Denim does not need to be lined. Unless your window is very wide, it looks good as a single curtain that can be drawn to one side.

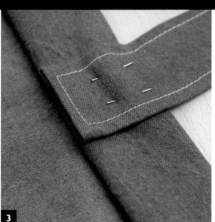

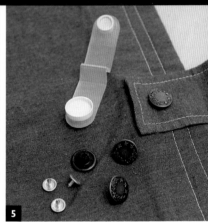

materials

Denim (see measuring up)
Jeans rivets and assembly tool
Yellow thread
Hammer
Sewing machine
Sewing kit

measuring up

This treatment hangs inside the window reveal, so measure the width and length of the window. Add an extra 6 in. to the length and 3 in. to the width for turnings. You will also need an extra 18 in. for the tab tops. Double-check your calculations.

1 Wash the denim before you begin to preshrink it and to soften the fabric. Cut the curtain to the size of your measurements. **2** Allow one tab for every 12 in. of the width. To make each tab, cut one piece of denim 13 x 4 in. Fold in half lengthwise, right sides together. Stitch across one short seam and along the long edges. Press the seams open. Trim the seams and corners. Turn right side out. Turn in the raw edge and slipstitch to close. Press. Topstitch all around each tab. **3** Turn in the seams around the raw edges of the curtain, mitering the corners. Press and slipstitch the miters. Pin the tabs at equal intervals to the wrong side of the top of the curtain. Baste. **4** Double topstitch all around the curtain, taking in the tabs. **5** Turn the free ends of the tabs to the curtain front and attach the rivets using the assembly tool and hammer.

accordion blind

This blind is made from a thick textured paper made in France, which folds very neatly. The green rectangles are made from an abaca tissue paper. This has wet strength and can be dyed quite easily. The rectangles are further embellished with ink stamps and fine black pen to create the 1950s-style design.

1 Cut long rectangles from the abaca tissue paper. Spray the pieces with adhesive and stick them to the pink paper in a random arrangement. **2** Draw a light pencil line lengthwise through each of the green rectangles at varying angles. **3** Transfer the stamp shapes from the templates on page 230 onto the neoprene sheet and cut out. Glue each shape to a block of wood. Mark the exact position of the shape on the reverse side of each block. **4** Use a sponge roller to ink the stamp with paint. Line up the stamp block with the pencil lines and print two or three stamps along each one. **5** Draw in the line between the stamps with the pen. Add details such as the spiky flower head, large dot, and small bar shapes. **6** Mark every 1½ in. down the sides on the back of the blind. Score across the blind between the marks with a blunt tool. **7** Fold the blind along the score lines to form an accordion. Join two pieces of accordion together to make a larger blind by overlapping the paper so that the cut edge tucks into the fold line. Glue in position. **8** Close the accordion and punch a hole 1¼–1½ in. from the side edges. **9** Following the chart on page 230, thread the fine white cord through the holes. Fit attractive beads at the bottom of the blind. Use the wood slat to attach the blind to the window frame.

1

4

5

9

materials

Pale pink Mi-tiente paper, cut to the width of the window

Pale green abaca tissue paper

Burgundy red acrylic paint

Fine white cord

Wooden slat to fit across the top of the window 2 in. wide

Two wood blocks ½ x ¾ x 2 in.

Wood panel ¼ x 2 in.

Panel pins and hammer

Large beads

Neoprene sheet

Fine black drawing pen

Wood blocks for the stamps

Scissors

Spray adhesive

Ruler

Pencil

All-purpose glue

Small sponge roller

Hole punch

beaded sheer curtain

The butterflies and marigolds drifting across this organza drape will draw everyone to admire the intricacy of the beading. This curtain is made to veil the window and wrap the light in a soft sheen. But the flash of color from its tiny glistening beads creates a subtle yet dramatic effect.

3

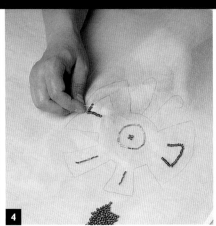

4

5

6

materials

**White organza
70 x 45 in. (or to fit window with
added seam allowance)
Twelve café curtain clips, or as
many as you need
Café curtain (tension) rod to fit the
width of the window
1¾ oz. of size 6/0 beads in each
color of red, pink, pale green, dark
green, pale blue, dark blue, yellow,
purple, and black
White thread
Soft lead pencil
Sewing machine
Sewing kit**

1 Photocopy as many flower and butterfly templates on page 231 as you want for your curtain. **2** Lay the organza right side up and slide the templates underneath in an arrangement of your choice. **3** Trace lightly over the templates with the pencil, then remove the photocopies. **4** Begin sewing beads over the lines with backstitch, completing each shape from the center out. **5** Sew the beads in place on all the flowers and butterflies, following the color key on the templates. Keep all threads and knots to the back, neat and tight. **6** Hem three sides with a ½ in. doubled hem pressed in place and sewn with a single row. Make the hem at the top of the curtain ½ in. to allow some leeway for clips. **7** Attach the clips along the top of the curtain. Keep an even spacing in between. Slip the clips onto the tension rod and insert into the window recess following the manufacturer's instructions.

knitted hemp curtain

This rugged hemp curtain mimics the display of old twine nets with hand-blown glass bobbers caught up in them hung in New England stores and restaurants. With its repeat pattern of a simple knit stitch, even the most unskilled knitter can approach it with confidence. You do not even purl one stitch!

materials

FINISHED SIZE 53 X 44 IN.

Twelve 3½ oz. balls of thin hemp twine (available from bead shops)
500 ½ in, frosted plastic beads in an assortment of colors and shapes
Net curtain wire kit for 46½ in., or to fit window
Pair of US size 11 (UK/CAN 8.0 mm) knitting needles
4 yd. of ½ in. wide linen binding tape
Linen thread to match the color of the tape
Sewing machine
Sewing kit

1 Knit a tension sample with some spare twine and adjust the pattern as required to fit your window. The finished size of this curtain is 53 x 44 in. Tension: 5 sts = 2 in.; 10 rows = 2 in. **2** Begin unrolling the first ball of twine by pulling the end from the middle of the ball: This keeps the twine from twisting. Pull out a workable length and then string on a random selection of seventy beads, leaving enough twine to cast on 120 stitches. **3** Cast on, drawing up and catching in a bead in the first stitch, and then every fifth stitch, ending with a bead in the last stitch. **4** Begin knitting the curtain. By knitting every row, the tension in the twine pulls back on itself, keeping the work flat. To create the bead pattern, add the beads in a random color sequence, beading every sixth row. **5** Begin the pattern by drawing up a bead and adding it into the knitting on the tenth stitch of the sixth row and then every tenth stitch across that row. Knit five more rows. On the twelfth row, begin beading the fifth stitch in the row and then every tenth stitch across the row. **6** Repeat this pattern up the entire length of the curtain, beading every sixth row and adding on additional balls of twine. Each time you begin a new ball of twine, draw out a workable length from the middle and string on about forty beads from a mixed bag. **7** You may need to adjust the distance of the beads and rows according to your tension and the measurements required. **8** When you are about 4 in. short of the top of the curtain you need to hang the knitted panel up to let it stretch. Without binding off the top edge of the curtain, pin the tail end of twine to the edge of curtain and leave the rest to hang down. Twist screw eyes into place at the inside top edges of the window frame. Cut the curtain wire to the correct width and slip the curtain from the knitting needle onto it. Screw on the hook ends and hang the curtain in place for at least forty-eight hours. **9** Readjust the length if necessary by unscrewing one hook from one end of the net wire and sliding the curtain back onto a knitting needle. Add on or take off as much as is needed to allow your curtain to hang to the required length. **10** To finish the top, slip the loops of the top edge back onto the curtain wire, and with a large-eyed needle and a length of hemp twine, sew in a running stitch across the top through the knit loops on the wire. Make two rows of stitches to keep the knitting secure. Alternatively you could run it through a sewing machine on a long basting stitch, sewing two rows. **11** To finish the edges, cut two pieces of linen tape to the length of the curtain, leaving enough for hems at the bottom. Hang the curtain up and pin each length of tape along the back edge of the sides. **12** Take the curtain down and stitch the tape in place on a sewing machine using a long basting stitch or by hand with a running stitch. Neaten and trim all the ends.

tulip screen

A three-fold screen can be cheered up with a collage of vibrant tulip panels. For a balanced appearance, make the bottom panels 4 in. deeper than those on the top two rows, and keep the same border around the panels except at the bottom—make that slightly deeper.

materials

Three-fold screen
Sugar paper in a range of colors
Handmade papers
Emulsion paint
Paintbrush
Tracing paper
Hard and soft pencils
Glue stick
Scissors
White school glue
Spray matte varnish

1 Enlarge one of the tulip templates on pages 232–233 and draw the outline onto tracing paper. **2** Transfer the shape onto the colored sugar paper for the main tulip. **3** Carefully tear along the pencil lines. To ensure that the torn edge remains neat and accurate, work with the first finger and thumb of both hands. Keep your hands close together and tear a short distance at a time. **4** Cut out a background panel to fit from the handmade paper. (Choose paler shades for the panels to complement the sugar paper tulips.) **5** Following the main photograph, tear out two leaf shapes and a stalk in green paper. Stick the leaves and stalk in place on the background panel. **6** Stick the main tulip piece to the top of the stalk. **7** Transfer the outlines of the petal shading to different colors of sugar paper and tear off. Stick these in place, beginning with the largest pieces and building up the layers until the smallest details are glued on top. **8** Complete nine panels in all, using three different background colors. **9** Paint the screen in a coordinating color. This screen was painted in a dull ivory and distressed to show the original sage green around the edges. Leave to dry. **10** Dilute the white school glue with an equal amount of water, and use to stick the panels to the screen. **11** Spray the screen with matte varnish to protect the surface.

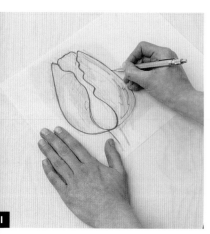

1

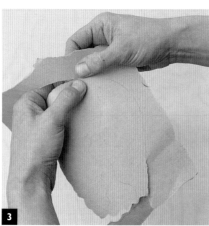

3

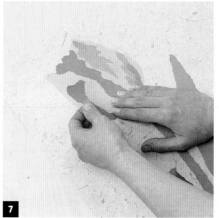

7

10

Many furniture items are handed down from generation to generation. Their pleasing proportions and strong lines are conducive to a whole range of decorative techniques, which can be used to give them a modern appeal and incorporate them into the general design scheme of a room. Their existing knocks and dents add interest and give them a greater sense of character. Bring together a disparate collection of kitchen chairs by painting them in the

same colors and giving them a crackle-glazed finish. Decorate chests of drawers with torn papers and weathered oak handles or a simple stenciled laurel-leaf motif. Brighten up an old cupboard with a classic checkerboard pattern and metallic paints. And rummage through kitchen drawers or a tool kit to find studs, nails, and tacks to protect the surface of a battered table.

furniture

studded coffee table

Roofing studs, nails, and tacks make an unlikely choice for decorative materials, but the combination of the natural colors of copper, steel, and galvanized metal gives this coffee table a wonderful contemporary appearance. The table itself is made from recycled floor joists with wheels for legs.

materials

Two hardwood floor joists or similar, 36 in. long

Four 6 in. castor wheels and screws to fix them

150 galvanized metal and/or copper roofing studs

650 clout nails

500 steel tacks

500 copper hardboard pins

Four 1½ in. metal box corners

Twelve tacks to fix the corners

24 x 8 in. plywood board

Twelve 1½ in. screws

Screwdriver

Electric drill and drill bits

Hammer

1 To decorate the top surface of the hardwood, hammer in the roofing studs 4 in. apart in three rows down the length of each board. **2** Hammer in the clout nails, making a circle of about twelve nails around each roofing stud. **3** Hammer in the steel tacks in a circle inside the clout nails. **4** Finally, hammer in the hardboard pins. Decorate the sides in a similar way. **5** Place the boards right side down, on a protected surface. Center the plywood on top. Make holes for the screws, then screw to secure. **6** Place a wheel at each corner and screw into position. **7** Screw the metal corners in place.

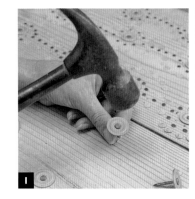

metallic-effect cupboard

Stripes and checks in shades of bronze, brass, and copper bring an old cupboard to life in an original way. By using all vertical stripes, rather than going with what looks like original drawer positions, the cupboard takes on more elegant proportions. The metallic paints give it a subtle sheen.

materials

Furniture to be painted
Selection of bronze powder, metallic pigments, or ready-mixed water-based metallic paints
Metallic car spray paint
Pale biscuit emulsion
Terra-cotta emulsion

Water-based eggshell varnish
Matte emulsion water-based glaze
Acrylic primer
Interior filler (if needed)
White school glue
Tracing paper
Pencil
Stencil cardboard
Ruler
Scalpel and cutting mat
Masking tape
Fine-grade sandpaper
Decorator's sponges
Selection of small brushes
Paint jars for mixing paints and glazes

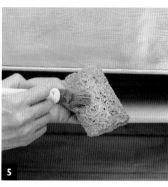

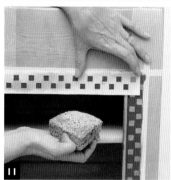

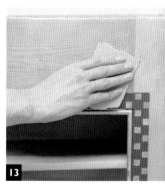

1 Draw a checkerboard onto tracing paper. Glue to stencil card. Using a scalpel, cut out the squares. **2** Sand the cupboard and fill in any holes. Allow to dry and sand flat. Mask out any glass panels. **3** Brush on a coat of primer and allow to dry. Add a coat of biscuit emulsion. **4** Mix one part terra-cotta with one part matte emulsion glaze and two parts water. Sponge over the cupboard inside and out. Use a brush to get into corners. **5** Add metallic powder to the white school glue and mix with a little water to a consistency slightly thicker than milk. Transfer the solution to a decorator's sponge with a small brush. Coat the cupboard inside and out. Allow to dry. **6** Mask the position of the first stripe. Mix a solution of differently colored metallic powders and glue and sponge on between the first masked lines. Allow to dry. **7** Remove the tape. Apply a new strip over the painted stripe so the second stripe can be washed up to the first. **8** Tape the position you would like the second stripe to end. **9** Make another metallic mixture and repeat. Cover the whole cupboard in stripes. **10** Using masking tape, mark a border around the glazed section and paint it in terra-cotta emulsion. **11** Paint a bright gold and glue mixture onto a decorator's sponge. Using the stencil, sponge on the border. Brush the gold over the beading. **12** Spray paint the inside of the cupboard. **13** Lightly sand the whole surface, then seal with a water-based eggshell varnish.

decoupage chest

Torn squares, rectangles, and triangles of recycled paper give an old chest of drawers a completely new look. A final coat of varnish lends a translucency to the papers and provides a protective finish. Paste on shapes layer upon layer until you are happy with the overall effect, adding as little or as much as you want.

materials

Chest of drawers
Pieces of weathered oak for drawer handles
Selection of papers such as brown paper, Japanese handmade paper, and tissue
Diluted cream emulsion
Acrylic primer
Dead-flat oil varnish
Fine sandpaper
White school glue
Ruler
Pencil
Scissors
Steel straightedge
Measuring tape
Small saw for trimming handles
2-in. bolts, one for each single handle, and two for the doubles
Washers and nuts to fit the bolts
Drill with bit to fit the bolt holes
Selection of brushes

1 Sand and prime the drawers. **2** For the decorative panels, measure the width and length of the drawer fronts and draw the dimensions onto your choice of paper. **3** Hold a straightedge against the drawn line and tear carefully. **4** Tear paper strips to cover the edges of each drawer. **5** Mark and tear or cut the applied shapes and patterns—for example, squares, strips, zigzags, and triangles. **6** Brush glue onto the back of each shape. Brush the drawer front with glue, then apply the first shape. Brush the drawer with glue and apply another shape, building up the layers. End with a final coat of glue. **7** In the same way, apply glue to the strips that will cover the drawer edges and stick into place. **8** Bring the edge piece neatly over the side, adding more paper if needed. Repeat until all the drawers are covered. **9** Use a similar method to cover the top and sides of the chest. Apply one large piece to completely cover the top or side, then apply the decoration. **10** Allow the drawers to dry completely, then brush the whole unit with dead-flat varnish. Allow to dry. **11** Trim the handles to size and sand down. Paint with diluted cream emulsion. **12** Drill ½ in. holes into the handles in appropriate places. Align with the screw holes on the drawers. Do not drill right through the handles. Apply glue to one bolt head, then push this into the handle. Place the handle bolts into the holes in the drawer front and fix at the back with a washer and nut.

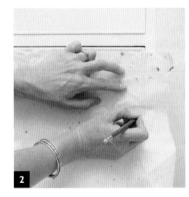

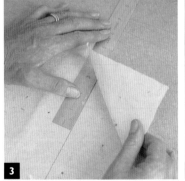

crackle-glazed chairs

The pretty, classic French shape of a set of rush-seated chairs has been given a fresh appeal with a soft Scandinavian blue paint effect. This easy-to-apply technique can be used to decorate and transform all types of wooden furniture with different intensities of "crackle."

 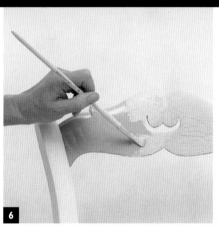 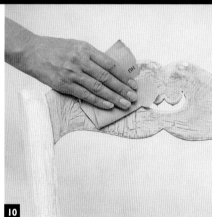 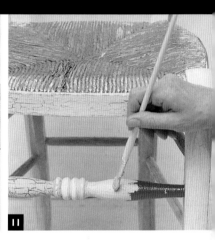

1 Prepare the chairs by sanding down the old finish. Remove any loose or flaky paint. **2** Fill any splits or holes. Allow to dry, then sand down any rough edges. **3** Mask off any areas not intended for painting. **4** Brush on a coat of acrylic primer and allow to dry. **5** Brush on a coat of the darker shade of eggshell. Allow to dry. **6** Lightly sand the first coat, then paint over with a lighter shade. **7** As soon as this is applied, mix up a pale emulsion with filler in quantities of two parts emulsion to one part filler. **8** Brush onto the chair while the previous coat is still tacky. **9** Apply heat immediately with a hair dryer and the crackles will appear. **10** Allow to dry thoroughly. Sand all the surfaces to give a distressed look. **11** Using a different base and top coat, repeat the process on different parts of the chair to add interest.

materials

Wooden chairs
Paint colors in eggshell finish, at least one darker shade for the first coat and a lighter shade for the top coat
Similar colors in matte emulsion but in paler shades
Interior-quality filler
Acrylic primer
Medium and fine grade sandpaper
Masking tape
Selection of small brushes
One paint jar for each color
Hair dryer

stamped blanket box

A traditional fleur-de-lis design, stamped in a formal pattern on each of the surfaces, combined with a contemporary, fresh color scheme of yellow and sage green transforms this functional blanket box into a stylish piece of furniture that can become a design feature of a bedroom.

materials

QUANTITIES GIVEN ARE APPROXIMATE AND DEPEND ON THE SIZE OF THE FURNITURE.

Blanket box or suitable wooden box
¼ gallon sage-green oil-based paint for the base coat
9 fl. oz. dark yellow paint in eggshell finish
Sample can of navy blue acrylic paint
Fleur-de-lis stamp (see step 1)
Small roller
Lining brush
1 in. brush
Pencil
Ruler
Masking tape
Sandpaper

1 Make a fleur-de-lis stamp using the template on page 235 or buy one from your local craft store (see page 10). **2** Sand off any flaking paint and old varnish from the surface of the box. Apply a base coat of sage green paint. **3** Using the pencil and ruler, measure and draw a border with indented corners on the front of the box. **4** Mask off the area and dry brush dark-yellow eggshell paint across the panel. Remove the masking tape carefully and immediately. **5** Lightly brush over the surface of the box with sage green, so that the yellow shows through. **6** Using the roller, apply navy blue paint to the stamp. Place the stamp in position at one corner and stamp firmly. Repeat at each corner. **7** Using a lining brush and blue paint, carefully add a blue line around the edge of each panel. Allow to dry. Repeat for the other sides and for the lid of the box.

laurel leaf chest of drawers

A chest of drawers can keep pace with changing tastes, with a new coat of paint and a little understated decoration. This pretty chest of drawers, perfect for a feminine bedroom, was lime washed before a laurel leaf design was stenciled onto it in a delicate shade of green.

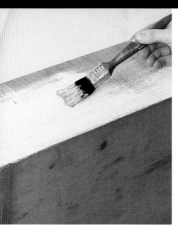 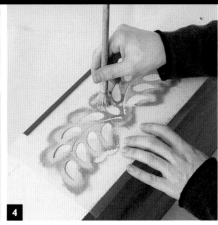  

materials

QUANTITIES GIVEN ARE APPROXIMATE AND DEPEND ON THE SIZE OF THE FURNITURE.

Wooden chest of drawers
¼ gallon lime white paint in eggshell finish for the base coat
Tube of light green acrylic paint
Tube of medium green acrylic paint
Stencil film
Stencil brush
2 in. brush
Lining brush
Craft knife and cutting mat
Pencil
Ruler
Masking tape
Sandpaper

1 Trace the laurel leaf template on page 234. Tape it to the cutting mat with the stencil film secured over the top and cut out using the craft knife. **2** Sand off any flaking paint and old varnish from the surface of the chest of drawers. Using lime white paint as a base coat, dry brush each side of the chest of drawers in the direction of the grain. **3** Using the pencil and ruler, draw a center line across the depth and width of each drawer as a guide for stenciling. **4** Position the leaf stencil. Using light green paint, flick the brush from the top of each leaf downward. **5** With medium green, stencil the stalk. Flick paint from the base of each leaf up. **6** Paint a border line in light green around the drawer front. Mask off the central leaf, position on each corner, and stencil as before.

mosaic tabletop

Create your own "mosaic" tabletop using the simple technique of stamping, without the bother of cutting glass, grouting, or using specialty tools. All you need is a mosaic tile–sized stamp and acrylic paint. This fresh blue/gray/lilac scheme looks stunning in a bathroom, kitchen, or sunroom.

materials

QUANTITIES GIVEN ARE APPROXIMATE AND
DEPEND ON THE SIZE OF THE FURNITURE.

Small wooden table
¼ gallon pale beige oil-based paint
for the undercoat
Tube of lilac acrylic paint
Tube of pale gray acrylic paint
Tube of pale blue acrylic paint
Tube of mid-blue acrylic paint
Mosaic tile stamp (see step 1)
Small brushes
Varnish
Cardboard
Sandpaper

1 Buy a mosaic tile stamp or make a stamp on foam rubber using the template on page 235 (see page 10). **2** Sand off any flaking paint and old varnish on the table, and apply a base coat of pale beige to the top. **3** Dab several colors of acrylic paint onto a piece of cardboard, being careful not to blend them together too much. **4** Dip the stamp in the paint. Starting at one corner of the tabletop, press the stamp down firmly. **5** Using the previous stamp as a guide, continue across the tabletop, leaving a "grout" line between each stamp. **6** For the edge, hold the top of the stamp at each end and print a line of "tiles" along the side. **7** Apply a final protective coat of varnish if the area you are working on is used on a daily basis.

plant stand

This plant stand, with its striking geometric pattern, takes its influence from pre-Columbian pottery designs, incorporating a simple, bold pattern that uses three shades of blue with a fiery orange/pink contrast tile. The combination of its slender height and dashing colors make a strong statement.

1 If possible, remove the top from the stand. Sand the edges and top to "key" the surface. Mix two parts white school glue with one part water and brush a thin layer over the top and sides. Leave to dry. **2** Photocopy the template on page 235. To enlarge, draw lines across the pattern to quarter the page, and enlarge each quarter page to get the correct size when pieced together. Tape all four copies together, carefully joining up the zigzag pattern. **3** Trace the pattern onto tracing paper and rub the back with charcoal. Place on the tabletop and draw over the pattern with a sharpened pencil. Remove the tracing paper and draw over the pattern again with the pencil. **4** Remove the backing paper from all the tiles. If the backing is mesh, just pull the tiles off; if the backing is paper, soak the tiles for fifteen minutes in water, then peel away the paper. Leave to dry. **5** Begin the pattern by first working the coral-pink tiles. With the tile nippers, cut a quantity of tiles in half and lay them out in position on the tabletop. Use the nippers to shape the tiles for the bends in the pattern and around the edges of the table. **6** Stick the tiles on by

"buttering" the backs with grout/adhesive spread on thinly with an artist's palette knife. Stick securely in position; keep all edges of tiles and the exposed surface of the tabletop clean of grout/adhesive as this will hinder the placement of the blue tiles. Leave to dry for a day. **7** Stick on the three shades of blue tiles in the same way, using the main picture as a reference. Leave to dry for twenty-four hours. **8** For the edge of the table, continue the color patterns on the top and stick on tile halves around the edge. Leave to dry for a day. **9** Spread waterproof grout over the tabletop and edges with a grout spreader. To facilitate working on the edges, raise the tabletop off your work surface—I used an upside-down pie dish. **10** Scrape all excess grout off the surface and smooth around the edging tiles top and bottom. Wipe with a damp sponge until the tile surfaces are clean, rinsing the sponge as you work. Smooth more grout around the table to give a finished edge and wipe smooth with the sponge. Leave to dry for twenty-four hours. **11** Wipe the tabletop with a soft cloth and apply a thin coat of clear floor wax to finish the surface.

3

6

7

9

materials

Wooden plant stand on metal base
with a 47 in. circumference, 14 in.
diameter, 1 in. thickness

One 14 in. square sheet each of
"Mazurka" range 1 in. square floor
tiles in cobalt blue, medium blue,
ice blue, and coral pink

Waterproof grout/adhesive

Tracing paper

White school glue

2 in. paintbrush

Adhesive tape

Charcoal

Sharp pencil

Protective goggles

Tile nippers

Artist's palette knife

Grout spreader

Sponge

Soft cloth

Clear floor wax

Sandpaper

upholstery tack chair

A straight-backed chair can be given a new look with this clever technique. Using a dot stamp dipped in a rough blend of bronze and black paint to stamp rows of "metallic" dots, you can create an apparently three-dimensional upholstery tack effect.

 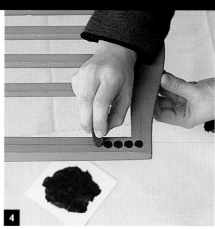 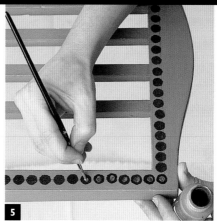 

materials

QUANTITIES GIVEN ARE APPROXIMATE
AND DEPEND ON THE SIZE OF THE FURNITURE.

Straight-backed wooden chair
¼ gallon dark-turquoise oil-based paint
for base coat
Tube of black acrylic paint
Tube of bronze acrylic paint
Tube of light bronze acrylic paint
Tube of gold relief paint
½ in. diameter circle stamp (see step 1)
Cotton reel
Sandpaper
Paintbrushes
Pencil and ruler
Glue
Palette

1 Make a dot stamp with a piece of foam rubber and glue it to an empty cotton reel for ease of handling (see page 10). **2** Sand off any flaking paint and old varnish from the chair. Apply a base coat of dark turquoise paint. **3** Draw a pencil guideline along the center of each strut. **4** Pour black and bronze paint onto a palette, without blending the colors too much. Dab the stamp into the paint and begin stamping over the line. Proceed along the line, placing each stamp up against the one before, keeping the spacing tight. **5** Using a small brush and light bronze paint, add a dot to each stamp. **6** To add highlights, add a dot of gold relief paint straight from the tube, just off-center over each stamp.

Linens give a home its sense of comfort. Cushions heaped on a sofa and plump pillowcases teamed with a disheveled duvet on a bed are all welcoming and soothing. Rather than embarking on an endless search to find soft furnishings and linens that exactly match your color scheme or provide the right color accent, it is much easier, and often cheaper, to make them yourself. Cushions closed with a simple buttoned flap or ties do not need a zipper and

can be made as efficiently by hand as by machine. White bed linen can be customized with a stencil in your favorite color. A machine-washable kitchen tablecloth can be appliquéd in an afternoon, and a plain square of fleecy fabric can be transformed into a beautiful throw with a delicate pattern of ribbon flowers embroidered across the surface.

linens

ice poppies bed linen

Stamping on fabric is one of the easiest and most immediate ways in which to brighten up and personalize bed linen. Choose a good one hundred percent cotton fabric, which will accept and fix the paint readily. It will also wash and wear well, giving you many years of use.

 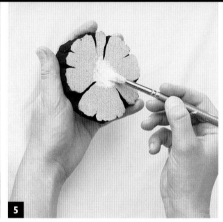  

materials

Single duvet cover and one pillowcase in white Egyptian cotton

Two small pots of pale blue fabric paint

Small pot of white fabric paint

Small pot of green fabric paint

Foam rubber

Small block of wood

Craft knife

All-purpose glue

Small roller

Cardboard

Container

Selection of artist's and stencil brushes

Masking tape

1 To make the flower-shaped stamp, transfer the template on page 234 onto foam rubber, cut out, and glue to the block of wood (see page 10). **2** Iron the duvet cover and pillowcase. Slip a piece of cardboard inside the pillowcase to avoid printing through both layers of the fabric. **3** Tape the edges of the pillowcase to the work surface to secure. **4** Pour a small quantity of pale blue fabric paint into a container, and using a roller, apply a thin layer to the surface of the stamp. **5** Apply white paint to the flower center using an artist's brush or stencil brush. Press the stamp firmly onto the fabric in the required position. **6** Repeating steps 4 and 5, randomly cover the surface of the pillowcase, allowing enough space between each flower for each of the stems. **7** With a fine artist's brush and green paint, paint the stem for each flower. **8** Complete the top surface of the duvet cover in the same way, but for the underside, apply closely spaced flower heads without stems.

lavender bags

This classically simple design in cool, crisp organdy has been tailored with French seams. Each bag is made to the same basic design, but one is fastened with two symmetrically placed mother-of-pearl buttons and the other is fastened with a silk cord couched into a heart.

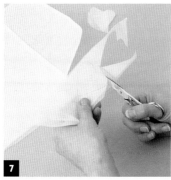

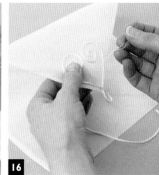

square-flap bag

1 For the square-flap bag, make a template 21¼ x 10¼ in. **2** Fold the organdy in half crosswise and pin the template along the straight grain, keeping the pins within a seam allowance of ½ in. Cut out through both layers and keep them pinned together. **3** On each long edge, measure 3½ in. from one end. Mark the point with colored thread in each seam allowance. Machine stitch around the edge of the organdy between the colored threads to form the bag flap. Stitch the other short end. **4** Trim the seam allowance to ⅛ in. Clip off the corners and turn through. **5** Press the seams flat. Fold the short, straight edge up to meet the start of the square flap and press the fold. Put aside. **6** Iron the fusible web to one side of a scrap of organdy. **7** Make a template of the heart on page 234 and cut out. Draw around it three times on the paper side of the web and cut out. Remove the backing paper. **8** Position the hearts on the bag front, between the two layers of organdy and just below the flap. Press to fuse the hearts in place. **9** Pin the side seams and stitch ¼ in. from the raw edge. Trim the seam allowance to ⅛ in. and press open as far as possible. **10** Turn the bag through and press flat. Stitch the side seams again ¼ in. from the edge. Sew in the thread ends. Turn the bag through and press. **11** Work running stitch around the edge of the hearts. Tie the ends off on the reverse side. **12** Mark the position of the buttons on the flap and work two buttonholes. Sew the buttons in the corresponding position on the bag front.

envelope-flap bag

13 For the braid work for the envelope-flap bag, make a template as for the square-flap bag 22½ x 10¼ in. Trace the template on page 234 and pin it to the organdy so that the point is in the center of one short end. Cut out. Make the bag up following the instructions for the square-flap bag. **14** Trace the braid-work design directly onto the organdy using a quilting pencil. **15** Fold the cord in two and pin around the lines, leaving a small loop to fasten the bag at the point. **16** Oversew the cord, stitching through the top thickness of organdy. Stitch the loop securely. **17** Oversew the cord several times at the end of the design and snip the cord close to the stitches. **18** Sew a toggle or button on the bag in the corresponding position.

materials

12 in. of 46 in. wide organdy
White silk embroidery thread
Fusible web
Paper
Pencil
Sewing machine
Sewing kit
Two small mother-of-pearl buttons
for the square-flap bag
20 in. silk cord for the envelope-
flap bag
Quilting pencil for the envelope-
flap bag
Toggle or button for the envelope-
flap bag

buttoned-up cushions

This cushion cover is elegantly tailored in the softest blue-colored linen and trimmed with four generous mother-of-pearl buttons. It has been lined with contrast ecru linen to give it a well-finished, immaculate look. It is put together like an envelope-style pillowcase; the cover is easy to remove for washing.

materials

Cushion pad, 12 in. square
24 in. of 45 in. wide blue linen
20 in. of 45 in. wide ecru linen
Four 1 in. diameter mother-of-pearl buttons
Blue sewing thread
Sewing machine
Sewing kit

1 From the blue linen, cut one 15 in. square for the cushion front and one 22½ x 15 in. piece for the back. **2** From the ecru, cut two pieces for the lining, one 15 in. square and one 15 x 7 in. **3** Turn in a double hem along one 15 in. edge on each ecru piece. **4** Stitch the opposite 15 in. raw edge of the square ecru lining to the blue square. Press. Fold on the seam line so that the wrong sides are together. **5** Place the blue rectangle, wrong side down, on a flat surface. **6** On top, at one end, place the blue and ecru panel. Align the raw edges. Pin. **7** Place the remaining ecru piece right side down on top, aligning the raw edges with the other end of the blue rectangle. Pin. There will be four layers of fabric at the center of the rectangle—blue rectangle, blue square, folded-over ecru lining, and ecru rectangle. **8** Ensure all the raw edges and the two hemmed edges of ecru are aligned. Baste around the raw edges. **9** Stitch around all four sides of the cushion, reinforcing the stitching over the overlap. Trim or overcast the seams. Remove the pins and basting stitches. Snip the corners off within the seam allowance to reduce bulk. Turn right side out. Press. **10** Position four buttons at equal intervals across the width of the cushion with their centers 3½ in. from the top edge of the blue square. Stitch each in position. **11** Fold the top flap down. Mark the corresponding position of the buttonholes. Machine stitch buttonholes to finish.

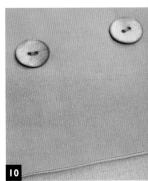

velvet stenciled cushions

Velvet is irresistible. Warm and soft to the touch, it feels gloriously extravagant, yet it is not vastly expensive, especially when you buy it in small, remnant-sized lengths. Its texture is emphasized here by the gold color and is decorated with a scattering of small motifs stenciled on in clear fabric paint.

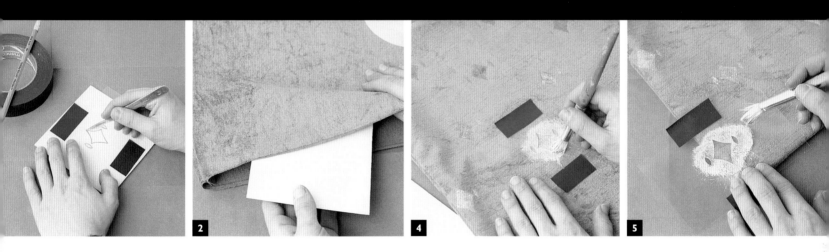

1 To make the stencil, trace or photocopy the templates on page 236. Tape to the cutting mat and secure the stencil film on top. Cut out along the lines carefully with the craft knife. **2** Slip a piece of cardboard inside the cushion cover to avoid printing through both layers of the fabric. **3** Secure the cushion cover by taping it to the work surface. **4** Position and secure each stencil, and stipple with clear fabric paint. **5** When stenciling at the edge of the cushion, position the stencil so that it overlaps the side and stipple as before. **6** Once the stenciling is complete and the paint is dry, sew the braid around the edges.

materials

Pair of "old gold" velvet cushions
Selection of braids
Sewing thread to match
Medium pot of clear fabric paint
Stencil brush
Stencil film
Craft knife and cutting mat
Masking tape
Cardboard
Needle

seaside tablecloth & napkins

The textures and colors of the seaside were the inspiration for this table linen, which combines the techniques of stamping and stenciling. The mood is restful and redolent of lazy days spent barefoot, combing the beach for shell souvenirs.

materials

QUANTITIES GIVEN ARE APPROXIMATE AND DEPEND ON THE SIZE OF THE TABLECLOTH AND NAPKINS.

Tablecloth and napkins in natural linen
Small pot of white fabric paint
Small pot of dark blue fabric paint
Foam rubber
Stencil film
Craft knife and cutting mat
Scissors
Masking tape
Cardboard
Small roller or paintbrush
Palette
Lining brush and stencil brush

1 Wash and iron the fabric to remove any dressing and to allow for shrinkage. **2** To make the stamps, transfer the outlines of the templates on page 237 onto foam rubber and cut out. **3** To make the stencils, trace or photocopy the templates. Tape to the cutting mat and secure the stencil film on top. Cut out along the lines carefully with the craft knife. **4** Place a piece of cardboard on a flat surface. Secure with masking tape. Smooth one of the napkins over the top and secure with more tape. **5** Pour a little white fabric paint onto the palette, and using a roller or paintbrush, apply a good amount onto one of the shell stamps. Place the stamp in position at the corner of the fabric and stamp firmly. Stamp all four corners, then position and stamp the slim shell border. Allow to dry. **6** Carefully place the shell stencil over the stamp. Dip the tip of the stencil brush in dark blue paint and flick inward from the edge of the stencil. Do not cover the white completely. **7** Using a fine brush and dark blue paint, add a line of definition around each shell. Repeat for the remaining napkins and the tablecloth to complete the set.

chenille drawstring bag

This exquisite bag can be made in any size as a cosmetics holder, lingerie or shoe bag, or even a large and luxurious laundry sack. The instructions would be the same, but larger bags would benefit from ready-made cord and tassels rather than handmade ones.

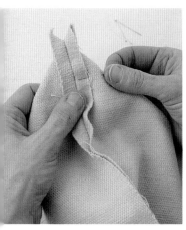
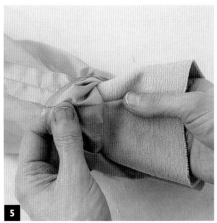
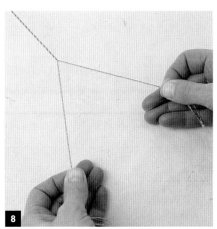

1 Cut two pieces of chenille for the bag and two pieces of silk for the lining, each 12 x 8 in. **2** Place the chenille right sides together. Machine stitch down the long sides and across one short side. Press the side seams open as far as possible. **3** To make the bag bottom, open out the corners and pinch the bottom seam to the side seam. Measure 1¼ in. down the side seam from the point and pin across. Machine stitch across the triangular point and turn through to the right side. **4** Make the lining in the same way, leaving a 2 in. gap along the short edge for turning later. Press the side seams open. **5** Tuck the chenille bag inside the lining, with right sides together. Match the seams and pin the raw edges around the top. Machine stitch ½ in. from the top raw edge. **6** Turn right side through, then slipstitch the gap. Tuck the lining inside the bag. Press the top edge flat. **7** Machine stitch a casing for the cord around the bag 2½ and 2¾ in. from the top edge. Snip into the stitching in the side seams between the two rows of channel stitching. **8** To make a cord, fold one skein of Marlitt thread in half and tie the ends to a door handle. Tuck a pencil into the loop at the other end. Holding the thread taut, rotate the pencil until the cord is tightly twisted. **9** Remove the cord from the handle, fold the thread in half, and tie the ends together. The two halves of the cord will automatically twist together. Run the cord between your finger and thumb to even out the twists. Cut the cord evenly in half and tie the ends to keep them from unraveling. **10** Use a bodkin to thread one cord around the bag, through the casing from one side, and back out of the same gap. Thread the second cord through from the other side. **11** Pull the two cords tight and tie a knot in each just below the bottom of the bag to form drawstring handles. **12** To make a tassel, cut a piece of cardboard 3½ in. square. **13** Wrap a skein of Marlitt tightly around the center of the cardboard, then snip the threads along one edge only. **14** Lay the threads out in a bundle on top of the cord ends so that the cut ends align. **15** Make one knot just below the midpoint. Tie a strong thread just above the knot to secure the threads. **16** Ease the threads around the cord evenly and then let them drop down over the knot. Wrap gold thread around the tassel below the knot to form a "neck" and tie off. Sew in the ends. Make a second tassel to match the first and trim the ends evenly, then sew to the ends of the drawstring handles.

materials

8 in. chenille velvet
8 in. Habotai silk
Three skeins of Anchor Marlitt thread
Gold thread
Bodkin
Pencil
Scissors
Cardboard
Sewing machine
Sewing kit

ribbon embroidery throw

Ribbon embroidery is a simple but effective way to decorate a soft woollen blanket or throw, and here only two stitches are used and the decoration is quick. The delicate blue and pink flowers are sewn with a lazy daisy stitch for the petals and sepals and French knots for the centers.

materials

Fleecy fabric
Offray embroidery ribbons, ⅛ in.
wide in 564, 571, 580
Offray embroidery ribbons, ½ in.
wide in 161, 168, 215, 303, 332, 345,
434, 447, 810
Open-weave linen for binding
Vanishing ink fabric marker pen
Ruler
Sewing machine
Sewing kit

1 Cut the fabric to the required size and square up the edges. **2** Fold the fabric in half and then in half again to find the center point. Mark the center point. Measure and mark every 4½ in. along the fold lines, stopping about 4½ in. from the raw edge. Fill in the grid of dots spaced every 4½ in. **3** At each dot work a lazy daisy stitch flower with five petals (see step picture). Keep the petals short so that the flower looks full. Choose the colors at random but avoid stitching two adjacent flowers in a similar color. **4** Work a lazy daisy stitch between each petal in a shade of green. Vary the green from flower to flower. **5** Work a French knot for the flower center using cream ribbon by winding the ribbon around the needle three times before taking it through to the reverse side. **6** Cut four pieces of linen 4½ in. wide and 4 in. longer than each side of the blanket. With right sides together, center the linen along each edge of the blanket 1½ in. from the raw edge. **7** Stitch the first piece of linen in place using a ½ in. seam, beginning and finishing 2 in. from the edge of the blanket. When sewing the second and subsequent pieces of linen, fold the previous piece out of the way and begin stitching at the same corner point, 2 in. from the edge. **8** Miter the corners on the right side and slipstitch in place. Trim the excess fabric. **9** Turn under ½ in. along the long edge of the linen. Fold over to the wrong side of the blanket as far as the stitching. Pin. Miter the corners on the wrong side and trim the excess fabric. Hem the linen to the machine stitching and slipstitch along the mitered edge to complete the throw.

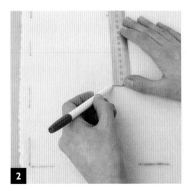

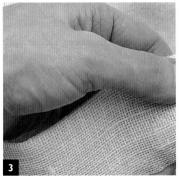

tied cushion

This is a simple cushion where the fastening has become the focal point of the design.
Ties can be made full like this, or slim and discreet, mimicking a traditional pillowcase.
The blue and neutral color combination gives the cushion a timeless elegance.

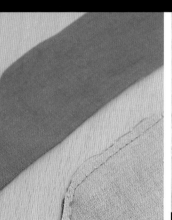
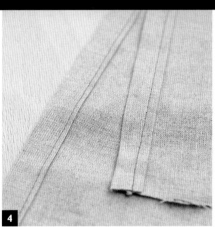
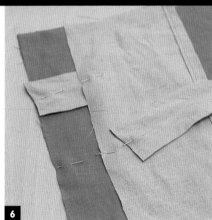

materials

12 in. square cushion pad
20 in. of 45 in. wide blue linen
12 in. of 45 in. wide ecru linen
Sewing thread to match
Sewing machine
Sewing kit

1 Cut two 15 in. squares from the blue linen. **2** Cut two rectangles 15 x 8 in. from the ecru linen. **3** To make the ties, cut four strips 20 x 3½ in. from the blue and ecru linen. Fold the top left corner of each tie down and trim away. Place one blue and one ecru tie right sides together. Stitch down the long edges and across the diagonal. Tidy the seams and turn right sides out. Press. Repeat to make four ties. **4** Turn in and stitch a hem along one long side of each ecru rectangle. **5** With pins, mark one side of one blue square into thirds. Place the marked-up blue square right side down on a flat surface. **6** Find the center of the raw edge of two ties and mark with pins. Match the pins with those on the cushion side and place blue side down. Align the raw edges. Place one ecru rectangle on top, aligning the raw edges. Stitch through all layers on this edge. **7** Press the seam open. Repeat with the other side of the cushion. **8** With right sides together and matching ecru sections, stitch along the cushion side, including the facing, along the short edge and the long edge. Press the seams open. Trim the seams and clip the corners. Turn right side out. Press. **9** Turn the facings in. Place the cushion in the cover, tucking it under the ecru facings. Tie to close.

secret color cushion

Plumped up on a sofa, this cushion offers subtle flashes of blue. Adapt the idea to make cushions in a range of shades picked out from the accent colors of the room. A simple opening center back means the cover can be taken off for cleaning without putting strain on the flange trim.

1

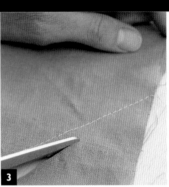
3

4

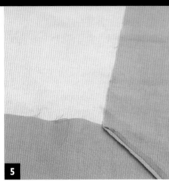
5

6

materials

12 in. square cushion pad
1 yd. of 45 in. wide ecru linen
½ yd. of 45 in. wide blue linen
Ecru thread
Sewing machine
Sewing kit

1 From the ecru, cut one square 19 x 19 in. Cut two rectangles 12 x 19 in. Stitch a double hem along one long edge of each rectangle. **2** From the blue, cut eight strips 19 x 4 in. **3** Place two strips right sides together. Fold down one corner until it meets the opposite side. Unfold and mark the line with pins. Machine stitch along this line and trim off the excess fabric. Continue joining the strips together with mitered ends to make two "frames" of four strips each. Press the seams open. **4** To make the cushion back to the correct size, place the ecru square right side down on a flat surface. On top, position the two ecru rectangles right side down and raw edges aligned. Overlap the rectangles at the center. Pin, then baste the overlap. **5** Separate the cushion pieces. Place one blue frame and the cushion front right sides together. Stitch around the outer edge. Repeat with the cushion back. Turn right sides out. Press. **6** Place the two sides of the cushion wrong sides together. Topstitch together through all thicknesses 2 in. from the edge around all sides. For emphasis, make another line of topstitching close to the first.

organdy tablecloth

This dreamy cloth veils the table, and glass beads sewn around the hem add sufficient weight to ensure the cloth lays flat. The understated elegance is achieved through the choice of organdy and glass beads, which are very close in translucency and color, so neither overshadows the other.

1 Square up the cotton organdy, and turn in and stitch a double hem all around. **2** Using double thread, make a stitch at one corner and thread on a round bead, a droplet bead, and two barrel beads. Add a tiny glass bead, then pass the thread over the last bead and back through all the other beads. **3** Pull the threads tight, then thread on another barrel bead. **4** Stitch the last bead to the right side of the cloth, at the corner. Finish off at the back. Secure the ends and repeat at the other three corners. **5** Using a similar method and beginning 4½ in. from one corner, thread on a round bead and a tiny bead. Pass the thread back through the round bead, then sew on a barrel bead at the hem and knot the thread. Repeat at regular intervals along the hem of the cloth.

materials

1¼ yd. cotton organdy
Sewing thread to match
Four glass droplets about ½ in. long
Forty-five round glass beads ¼ in. long
Ninety-six barrel-shaped glass beads ¼ in. long
Forty-five tiny round glass beads
Beading needle
Sewing kit

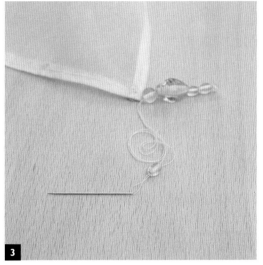

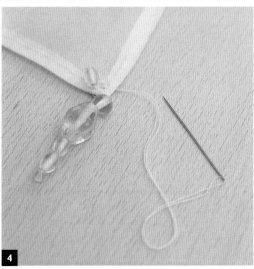

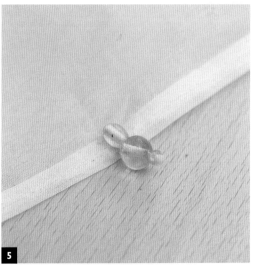

fishy appliqué cloth

Clean, uncluttered appliqué shapes, such as these fish and reeds, bring a fresh new look to traditional appliqué. A two-color design provides a smart and useful way to incorporate the joining of fabric widths to make up whatever size of tablecloth you need.

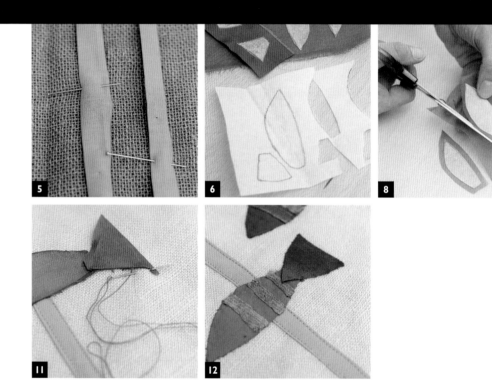

materials

1½ x 1¾ yd. yellow linen
1 x 1¾ yd. aqua linen
Selection of silks and organzas
Sewing threads to match
Fusible web
Sewing machine
Sewing kit

1 Cut two 12 x 60 in. strips of aqua linen. **2** Stitch a strip of aqua to each 60 in. edge of yellow. Press the seams open. **3** Turn in and stitch a double hem all around the cloth. **4** From scraps, cut reeds 1 in. wide in varying lengths. **5** Turn in the edges and pin in place. Stitch. **6** Make fish shapes using the templates on page 236. Transfer onto the paper backing of the web, leaving a large gap around each. **7** Cut out each and place web side down on the wrong side of silks and organzas. Fuse together following the manufacturer's instructions. **8** Cut out each shape, leaving a ¼ in. allowance all around for turning. **9** Turn in the edges of each piece. Clip the corners and curved edges where necessary to create a smooth shape. **10** Place the fish on the cloth in the desired pattern. Using matching thread, slipstitch in place. **11** Add the tails. **12** To add detail to the body, cut bands of contrasting colors ½ in. wide. Turn in the edges and slipstitch in place.

painted floorcloth

This painted floorcloth is an inexpensive solution to flooring and looks wonderful on bare floorboards. Paint it in your favorite shades, and when you are ready for a change, just sand it down, wash on an undercoat, then paint it in a set of fresh colors.

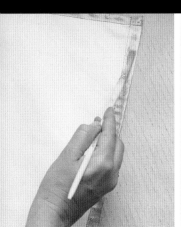 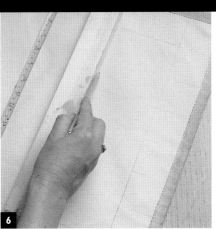 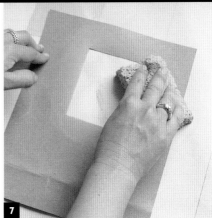 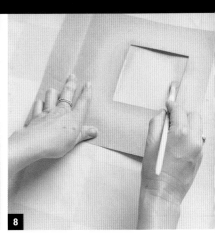

1 Some suppliers of cotton duck will prime and turn in the edges for you. If you choose to do this yourself, first wash the floorcloth, then prime it with watered-down acrylic primer. When completely dry, turn in and stitch a hem. **2** Dilute the paler emulsion one part paint to two parts water and one part matte emulsion glaze. **3** Coat the surface of the floorcloth with the solution using a sponge. Leave to dry. Apply a second coat using a large paintbrush. **4** Paint a dark border around the cloth using a small brush. **5** Determine the size of the border rectangles and the checkered squares. Make a stencil for each of these (see page 10). **6** On the floorcloth, lightly draw out a grid with squares corresponding to the size of the stencils. **7** Using the stencil and sponge and beginning at one corner, apply the second paint to alternate squares to create a checkerboard effect. Continue until all the squares are complete. Repeat with the other color. **8** Enhance the color of each square using a brush. Start at the edge of each square and work the color in toward the middle to give a shaded effect. **9** Lightly sand the surface of the cloth with fine sandpaper. **10** Varnish with matte acrylic to finish.

materials

Artist's cotton duck canvas, primed
with edges turned in
Emulsion paints in two toning colors
Matte emulsion glaze
Tracing paper
Pencil
Stencil card
Scalpel and cutting mat
Decorator's sponge
Large paintbrush
Small brush
Ruler and pencil
Measuring tape
Fine sandpaper
Matte acrylic varnish

A home cannot be a restful place if it is filled with junk and clutter. Storage items are an essential feature of any modern household, and by making them

yourself, you can design these items to suit your needs. The projects in this chapter are all designed to be attractive as well as functional, so they can

be on display while hiding things away. The tensile strength of corrugated cardboard has been put to good use in such projects as a magazine rack, a

laundry basket, and a group of graded sized pots. The structure of a crocheted wastebasket is strengthened by the interwoven chunky beads, rendering it attractive enough to be used in either a lounge or study. A pretty metalwork template decorates the mesh panel of a cheese larder, and a turtle mosaic graces the front of a plain bathroom cabinet.

storage

magazine rack

Made entirely from corrugated cardboard, this magazine rack is surprisingly solid when assembled. It may seem daunting to cut out so many pieces of cardboard but the template has been made so that each shape butts against the previous one, thereby reducing the required cutting by almost half.

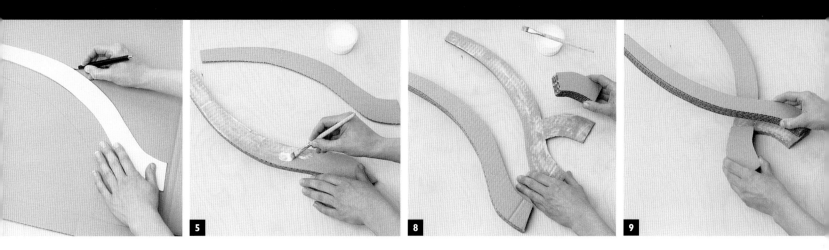

materials

Single-ply corrugated cardboard
Thick card stock
Pencil
Craft knife and cutting mat
White school glue
Adhesive tape

1 Transfer the template on page 238 onto thick card and cut out the two pieces. Mark the grain line across the center of the large card stock template. **2** Lay the larger template on the corrugated cardboard, matching the grain line to the corrugated flutes in the cardboard. Draw around the template, then move it across and down slightly so that the curve of the template butts against the previous shape. Draw around the template again. **3** Continue moving the template and drawing around it until you have five shapes, then begin again in another area of cardboard. This ensures that the corrugated pattern inside the cardboard looks the same on each piece. **4** Cut around the shapes with a craft knife. Cut sixty-eight large pieces altogether. Replace the blade on the craft knife regularly to prevent the fluting from tearing. **5** Stick five large pieces of cardboard together with the glue to make one bundle. Repeat until you have created twelve bundles of five pieces each. Stick the remaining eight pieces together to create two bundles of four pieces each for the end sections. **6** Cut and paste sixty-eight pieces in the same way with the smaller template. **7** Tape the large and small templates together again to make an inverted Y shape. Use this to draw and cut two shapes from the cardboard. **8** Paste one of the Y shapes and stick a bundle of four small and four large pieces to it to make an end section. **9** Position a large bundle over this to form a wishbone shape and mark the outline. Paste within the lines and stick in place. Stick a small bundle beside this to complete the next layer. **10** Continue building the layers until there are seven bundles on each side. Finish with two bundles of four and paste on the Y shaped end piece.

wastebasket

It doesn't take much to become accomplished at crochet with a little patience. By incorporating alternating colors of large wooden beads into a striped pattern of red, orange, and natural twines using double crochet, this wastebasket has a homespun quality that could easily blend into many interiors.

materials

**1 lb. ball of natural garden twine
5 oz. ball of dyed jute twine in each
color of red, dark orange, and pale
orange
Large-eyed sewing needle
US size 4 (UK/CAN 3.5 mm) crochet
hook
Eighty-four ½ in. diameter wooden
beads in colors of natural, pink,
orange, and red**

1 Using the natural twine, chain five stitches; join together with a slipstitch. Double crochet twice into every stitch, placing a colored string for a marker at the join. Work double crochet stitch once into every stitch; from then on every other row is an increase row. Work double crochet throughout. Make the increases by first increasing every other stitch by one stitch, then the next increase row every third stitch, the next increase row every fourth stitch, etc. This will keep the disk shape enlarging evenly and flat. **2** Crochet the base to 9½ in. across. Place a marker at the finishing point. **3** Begin the sides by crocheting one double crochet into every stitch along the edge. Turn the work so that the crochet hook faces you and work in the opposite direction to which the base is worked. Make five

rows in double crochet and cut off leaving a tail. **4** Take the ball of red twine and string twelve beads in two alternating colors onto the twine. Attach to the tail of the natural twine and continue the sides using double crochet according to the following pattern: three rows red—bead the middle row; one row light orange; one row natural; one row dark orange—bead row; one row natural; one row light orange; three rows red—bead the middle row; three rows natural. For the beaded rows, work a bead into every sixth stitch by drawing up one bead and making a stitch behind it. **5** Repeat the pattern. Finish off the top edge by crocheting a slipstitch around the rim. Cut off and work in the end.

storage bin

This large bin, covered with sections from a map, will hold all the oversized odds and ends of a busy family room or study. Look for an attractive map in the travel section of your local bookstore, then ask for it as a "flat" map. This comes rolled rather than folded, and so has no crease lines.

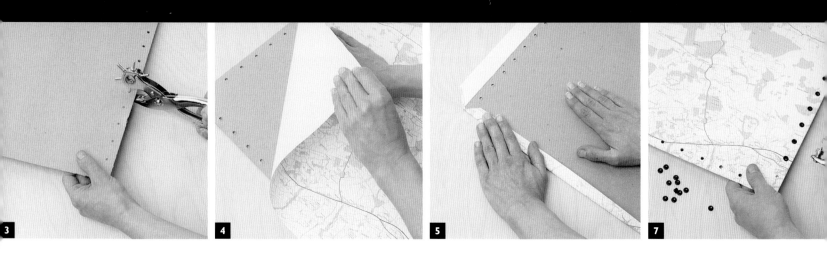

materials

Dense millboard ¹⁄₁₆ in. thick
Large flat map
Soft green paper
Soft green cord
Spray adhesive
Eyelet punch and eyelets
Assembly tool
Pencil
Craft knife
Ruler or steel measuring tape
Adhesive tape

1 Decide on the size of the bin. Cut four rectangular panels from the millboard and a square with sides slightly narrower than the short sides of the rectangles. **2** Draw a line ½ in. in from the edge down the long sides of the rectangles and along one short side and around each side of the square base. **3** Punch holes every 1¼ in. along the pencil lines. Make the holes just large enough to fit the eyelets. **4** Cut the map into four rectangles and trim to ½ in. larger than the board. Spray adhesive onto the back of one of the maps and one of the boards. Position the map on the board, press down, and smooth out any air bubbles with your hand. **5** Turn the board over. Trim across the corners of the map, spray the edge of the board with spray adhesive, and then fold the edges of the map over and stick in place. Repeat for the other three side panels. **6** Cut the green paper to fit on the back of the four side panels, overlapping the raw edges of the map. Spray the paper with adhesive and stick down. **7** Punch the holes through from the right side with a pencil. Push eyelets into the holes and use an assembly tool to secure. **8** Wrap a piece of tape around the end of the green cord. Feed the cord through the holes to "sew" two side panels together. Leave enough cord to join along one bottom edge and cut off. **9** Wrap a second piece of cord with tape and sew the third and fourth panels in position. Use the excess cord to attach one side of the base at a time. Tie the cord off neatly on the inside.

laundry box

Wide strips of painted corrugated cardboard have been woven together to make this large, sturdy box. Large sheets of corrugated cardboard can be obtained from packaging companies, or ask at local art stores that have mat board delivered in large, flat packs of plain cardboard.

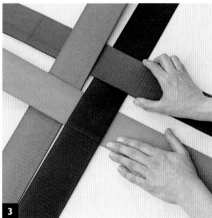
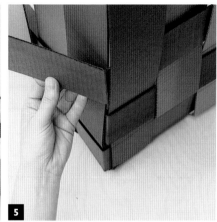

1 Cut twelve 3 in. wide strips from the cardboard with the grain running lengthwise. Cut another twelve strips with the grain running across the width. Cut all the strips at least 56½ in. long. **2** Dye two of each type with a different color of wood dye. Work in a well-ventilated room. Paint dye on both sides of the strips and allow to dry. **3** To form the base of the box, weave six strips (alternating colors) in one direction and six perpendicular so that the long ends stick out from a central woven panel. Use the strips with the grain running lengthwise if you want the grain on the finished box to run in the same direction. **4** Crease the strips at the edge of the panel and fold upright to begin to form the box shape. **5** Using the remaining strips, weave one strip of cardboard through the uprights, crease to go around the corner, and work in the next side. Use clothespins to temporarily support the uprights. Once the second and third strips are in place, the box will have a little more stability. **6** Keeping the same color sequence, weave a strip through the uprights and around the opposite corner. **7** Join the strips together on the inside by trimming the ends to overlap by 3 in. and gluing together. If the cardboard is bulky, tear away one layer from the end of each strip before gluing. **8** Continue weaving the sides in the same way until there are six horizontal strips. Fold the upright strips over the top horizontal strips. Alternate strips will fold to the inside and outside edges. Cut each flap to ¾ in. **9** Using the needle, punch two holes 1 in. apart in the middle of each upright just under the top flap. Oversew the yellow paper string diagonally around the top edge, going into each hole and the gap between the uprights. Sew in the end of the string through the cardboard and snip off. **10** Oversew the red paper string diagonally in the opposite direction. **11** Stitch the orange thread vertically and then make a running stitch along to the next hole. Continue working vertical stitches over each hole and running stitches between them. Complete the stitch pattern by working orange running stitch around the top to fill in the gaps. **12** Paint the entire box with two coats of matte acrylic varnish.

materials

Single-ply corrugated cardboard
Wood dyes in red, orange, yellow, green, blue, and purple
Paper string in yellow, red, and orange
Paintbrush
Craft knife and cutting mat
White school glue
Clothespins
Large-eyed needle
Matte acrylic varnish

mosaic cabinet

A Mosaic is not difficult to do and this delightful turtle mosaic brings charm and interest to an unassuming bathroom cabinet. The unusual combination of brick red, sage green, and blue matte tiles are set off by the iridescent glass tiles in the turtle shell.

materials

Square cabinet 14 x 14 in.
Sheet of 12 x 12 in. green glass mosaic tiles
Sheet of 12 x 12 in. tan glass mosaic tiles
Three sheets of 4½ x 4½ in. blue matte mosaic tiles
Three sheets of 5 x 5 in. terra-cotta matte mosaic tiles
Four sheets of 4½ x 4½ in. sage green matte mosaic tiles
Combined adhesive and grout for ceramic wall tiles
Paint
Paintbrush
Fine felt-tipped pen
Cardboard
Glue stick
Scissors
Spring-loaded tile nippers
Tweezers
Protective goggles
Sandpaper
Bowls
Palette knife
Sponge
Squeegee
Soft cloth

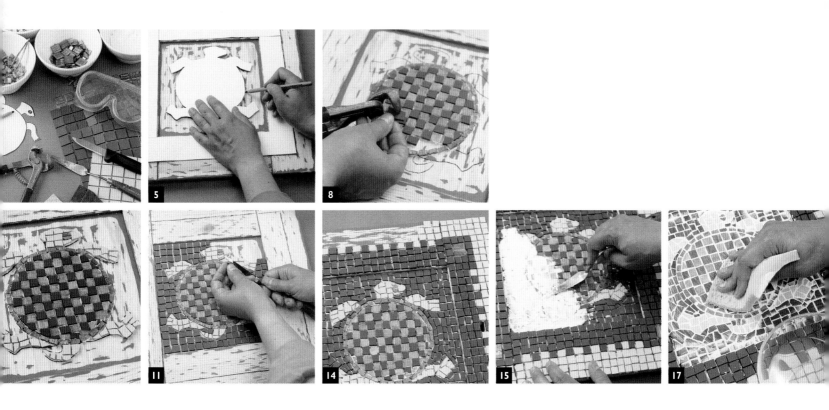

1 Wearing goggles for protection, snip the tiles roughly into quarters. Place them in color-graded bowls. 2 Sand the door of the cabinet. Scoring will help secure the tiles to the surface. 3 Photocopy or trace the template on page 236. Enlarge to fit the cupboard door as required. 4 Glue the template to cardboard and cut out. 5 Place the cardboard template on the cabinet door and draw around it with a pen. 6 With the nippers, cut the tan glass tiles for the outside edge of the turtle into thin rectangles. 7 Spread grout/adhesive onto the back of each tile and place it on the circle line. Continue until the circle is complete. 8 In the same way, fill in the turtle shell, working in lines from top to bottom. Use alternate green and tan quarter tiles. Cut individual pieces to fit at the edges. 9 Using the tile nippers, cut two small and irregularly shaped tan pieces to make the turtle's eye. 10 Fill in the head, tail, and legs with matte sage green tiles, clipping and adhering each one as you need it. 11 Fill in the turtle background with blue matte tiles. 12 For the outside border, fill in the terra-cotta key design. 13 Add the bold matte blue squares at the corners, then complete with tan glass tile centers. 14 Fill in the outside edge with sage green tiles. 15 Using a palette knife, thoroughly coat the tiled surface with the grout/adhesive, working it in well between the tiles. 16 Use a squeegee to remove most of the surplus and to push the grout between the tiles. 17 Use a damp sponge and plenty of water to wipe the surface clean. Dry with a soft cloth. 18 When the grout is completely dry, neatly fill in the gaps around the outside edge of the mosaic using a palette knife and grout/adhesive. 19 Allow to dry for about an hour, then wipe clean with a damp sponge. 20 Paint the cabinet sides, top, and bottom to match the door.

shoe boxes

We all have several pairs of special shoes that are kept in their original boxes until the proper occasion. These boxes are not particularly sturdy. Strong basic storage boxes, however, can be purchased from discount stores and transformed with this stunning cutwork design.

materials

Sturdy cardboard shoe-size boxes
Reproduction flat paint
Paintbrush
White paper
Carbon paper
Pencil
Craft knife and cutting mat
Tracing paper
Round file
Acrylic varnish

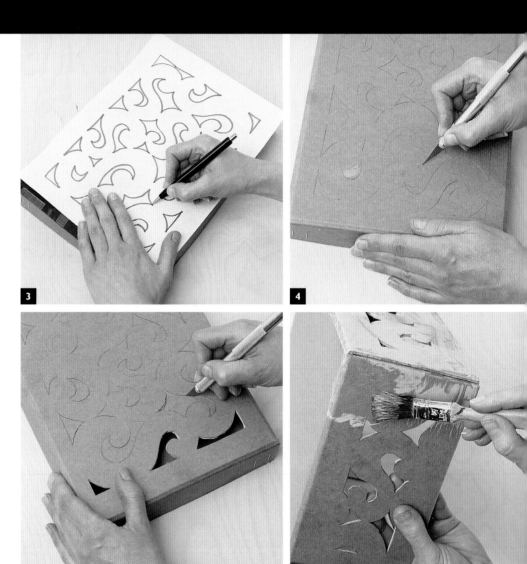

1 Enlarge the template on page 237 to fit the lid of the box, allowing a 1 in. border all the way around. **2** Lay the carbon paper, carbon side down, on the lid and position the template on top. **3** Holding the template firmly, draw around the lines of the design to transfer it onto the box lid. **4** Score along the lines using a craft knife. Use a long narrow blade to follow the curves of the pattern. **5** Cut into the cardboard along the score lines. Use the tip of the craft knife to go smoothly around the curves. Replace the blade frequently. **6** Cut pieces of tracing paper to the same size as the side and end panels of the box. Draw in a 1 in. border on each piece. Position your tracings over the main template and trace off a design. Transfer the lines to the side and end panels. Score and cut in the same way as before. **7** Paint the shoe box inside and out. Once dry, file the cut shapes to smooth any ragged edges. Paint the box with a second coat of paint. **8** Paint the box inside and out with a coat of acrylic varnish.

letter chest

There are many simple, well-designed cardboard accessories in stores today that are generally sold unassembled and can be folded to make durable, practical storage items for the home. Specialty stamp stores sell large packs of mixed stamps that are suitable for decoupage.

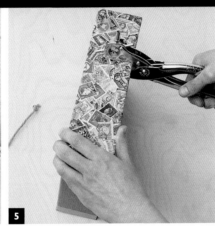

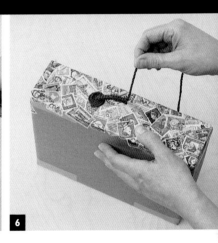

materials

**Three-drawer chest made of
corrugated cardboard
Stamps
Thick paper string
Blue medium paper string
Brown gummed tape
Wallpaper paste
Hole punch
Scissors
All-purpose glue
Pen
Matte acrylic varnish**

1 Make up the cardboard chest with the smooth side to the outside. Cover the slots and corner folds with the tape so that the surface is completely smooth. **2** Paste stamps on the front of the drawers. Dot the stamps all over the surface before beginning to fill in the gaps. This keeps the stamps from spiraling out from the one point and gives a more random appearance. **3** Stick stamps over the edges and about 2 in. down the sides. **4** Cover the sides and dividing panels of the chest in the same way, sticking the stamps about 2 in. inside. **5** Mark the position of the handles on the front of the drawers. Punch a hole at each marking. Tie a knot in the end of the paper string and thread through one hole from the inside. Thread back through the other hole and tie off on the inside. Trim off the excess string. **6** Spread glue around one hole on the front of a drawer. Working from the middle of the handle outward, wrap the blue string tightly around the handle, catching in the end as you go, and coil it around the hole to the required size. Trim the end. Unravel the string slightly, tuck the threads under the coil, and hold until the glue dries. Complete the other side of the handle in the same way. Repeat for each drawer. **7** Paint the chest with matte varnish.

cheese larder

A combination of wirework and metalwork techniques has been used to create the attractive front of this cheese larder. You do not need to search far in antique or junk shops to find an inexpensive old food cupboard that will lend itself to this project, which draws on the design of traditional pie safes.

materials

Twisted copper wire made with 14 gauge (0.06 in.) wire
Twisted copper wire made with 18 gauge (0.04 in.) wire
Flattened loops made with 14 gauge (0.06 in.) copper wire
Flattened loops made with 18 gauge (0.06 in.) twisted copper wire
A small roll of fine (24 gauge) copper binding wire
18 gauge (0.04 in.) copper wire
Wire cutters
Bent-nose pliers

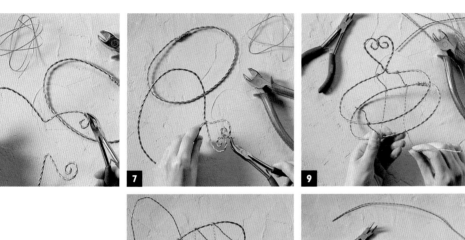

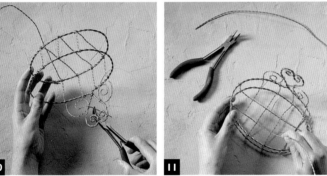

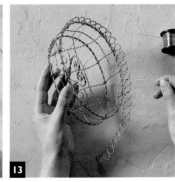

1 The copper wire should be twisted as you need it. (See page 11 for details on twisting.) **2** Cut two pieces of 14 gauge twisted wire, one 17 in. and one 26 in. **3** Form an oval with the short length and temporarily bind the two ends together with 18 gauge wire. **4** Form the second length into a similar-sized oval. Turn back each end at a 45° angle. **5** Using pliers form the ends into inward-facing spirals. **6** Push the spirals together to form a heart and bind tightly together with 18 gauge wire where the spirals touch and again at the base of the heart. **7** Bend the heart up so it sits at right angles to the oval. **8** Cut two lengths of twisted 18 gauge wire 12 in. long. Attach one end of each wire to each side of the heart by twisting the wire end twice around the twisted wire of the oval. **9** Twist the wire around the second oval 2½ in. away. Continue the wire under the base and up the opposite side, twisting around the ovals as you come to them. The oval with the heart shape will be suspended 2½ in. above the plain oval. **10** Cut two lengths of twisted 18 gauge wire 18 in.

long. Form one end of each into a small spiral. Attach each spiral facing inward, at the base of the heart. Continue to weave each wire around the oval frame, finishing at the top of the opposite side. Trim any excess wire. **11** Cut two lengths of twisted 18 gauge wire 18 in. long. Weave these wires across the oval frame, working at a right angle to the previous holding wires. **12** Cut one length of twisted 18 gauge wire 20 in. long. Weave this length around the walls of the basket. Twist neatly around one of the upright wires to finish. **13** Cut a 14 in. length of flattened twisted coils made from the thinner wire. Beginning at the side of the heart, bind the loops onto the top rim using fine wire. **14** Cut a 17¾ in. length of the larger coils made with untwisted wire and bind them around the base using fine wire. As you reach the join on the base oval, remove the temporary binding and replace it with finer wire. Trim the excess coils at the point of overlap.

coil pots

Rather than using clay, these coil pots have been created with strips of corrugated paper. The pleasing effect is achieved by overlapping pieces of torn white tissue paper that are pasted in layers over the surface to produce pots that are remarkably strong.

materials

Corrugated paper
White tissue paper
Craft knife and cutting mat
Ruler
White school glue
Matte acrylic varnish

1 Cut several ½ in. wide strips from the corrugated paper with the ribs running across the width. **2** Coil the corrugated paper, brushing white school glue on the rib side of the strips as you go. Keep the coil flat to form the base of the pot. **3** Allow the base to dry flat. Brush glue around the top half of the edge of the base and wrap a new strip of corrugated paper around it, sticking it down onto the glued section smooth side out. **4** Continue gluing and wrapping strips to form the bowl. The shape can be adjusted by overlapping the coils to different depths. **5** Once the coiled pot is the desired shape and size, level out the top by gluing the corrugated strip down onto the last full circle. **6** Pull the last ½ in. of the corrugated "flutes" away from the paper backing and glue down flat. Stick the backing over the rim to give a smooth finish. **7** Tear pieces of white tissue paper into long ragged shapes. Use diluted glue to paste the tissue paper in layers over the entire surface of the pot. **8** Once dry, paint with two coats of matte acrylic varnish.

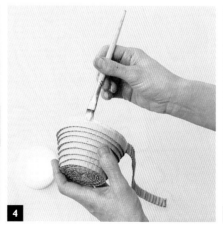

rose storage basket

Basic mesh and wire-framed stacking boxes can be made to look more decorative with the addition of handmade silk-ribbon roses. The flowers are deceptively simple to make—use soft gathers to begin with to form the bud and then increase them to form a beautiful full-blown rose.

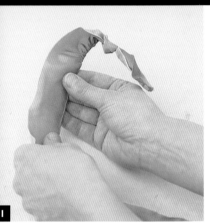
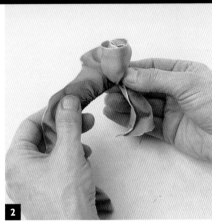
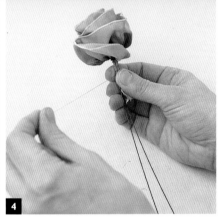

materials

Set of scrim boxes
1½ in. wire-edge ribbon, ombré and plain
Wired silk rose leaves
Florist's wire
Florist's green tape
Scissors

1 Cut a 36 in. length of ribbon and tie a knot in one end. Pull up the wire from the other end to make the ribbon gather. Gather the ribbon less near the knot and more at the start. **2** Hold the knot like a stem and wrap the ribbon around it to form a rose. **3** Tuck the raw edges of the ribbon between your fingers at the rose base, then wrap the pulled wire around to secure. **4** Fold a piece of florist's wire in half and secure the loop end to the ribbon stem with the uncovered wire. Continue wrapping the stem down the florist's wire. **5** Wrap 2 in. of stem below the rose with florist's tape. Stretch the tape as you twist the stem around until it sticks to itself. **6** Arrange two small rose leaves on a medium-sized one. Position the leaves behind the rose. Fold up the bottom of the rose stem if it is too long and finish wrapping the stem with florist's tape. **7** Mold the edge of the ribbon to form the rose shape. Open out the leaves and curve slightly. **8** Make the buds using a 10 in. length of ribbon. Gather the ribbon slightly before wrapping around the knot, and add a stem and three small leaves as before. **9** Thread two or three roses and one or two rosebuds into each side of the basket as desired. Overlap the stems on the inside and push the ends back through the scrim to secure them firmly.

twisted wire hook rack

This wire hook rack is designed with a dual purpose—to be attractive enough to be on display and to be sturdy enough to hold small tools in one place. Each flower is fashioned from a single piece of galvanized wire, then wrapped in fine silver or copper wire before being attached to the rack framework.

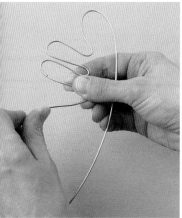

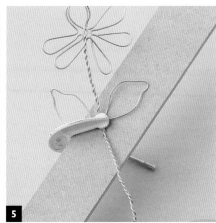

14 gauge (0.06 in.) galvanized wire
24 gauge (0.02 in.) silver-plated jewelry wire
24 gauge (0.02 in.) copper jewelry wire
Wire cutters
Parallel pliers
½ in. thick block of wood
Two C clamps
Hand drill
Masking tape
Large nail
Hammer

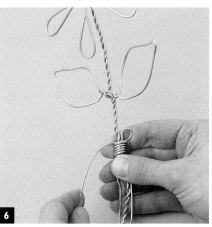

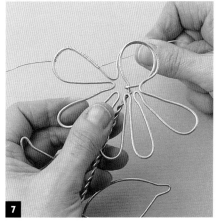

1 Cut a 2⅓ yd. length of galvanized wire. Beginning 6 in. to one side of the center, bend the long end of the wire into five continuous petals. Use your hands for the softer curves and the pliers for tight bends. **2** Bring the two ends together to make a rounder flower head using a double thickness of wire. **3** Secure the flower head upside down on the block of wood using a C clamp. Hold the galvanized wire halfway down each length and twist together to make a 3½ in. long stem. **4** Bend the wire to form a leaf on each side of the stem. Using pliers, twist each leaf around close to the stem. **5** Secure the stem with the C clamp again and continue twisting for another 3½–4 in. **6** Bend the wire straight back up on both sides. About 2½ in. from the end of the stem form a small loop on one side for a screw. Wrap the other wire around the stem five or six times and snip both ends. Bend the end up to form a hook. **7** Wrap each flower petal except the top one with silver wire. Use 36 in. lengths of wire and begin in the middle, using one half of the wire for each side of the petal. **8** Wrap the top petal and leaves in

the same way using a 40 in. length of copper wire. **9** Finally, snip the ends off on the reverse side. Make two more flowers. **10** Cut a 2¼ yd. length of galvanized wire and wrap the ends with masking tape. Put both ends into the chuck of the drill and tighten. **11** Hook the other end around a large nail secured into the block of wood. Turn the drill handle to twist the wire until it looks the same as the stem. **12** Bend a loop in the twisted wire about 10 in. from one end and another 3¼ in. away to make one end of the wire rack. **13** Bend the wire back up 14¼ in. along and make the other end to match. **14** Overlap the ends and find the center. Unravel the ends of the wire and twist one end on each side around to secure. Trim the ends. **15** Place the flowers on the wire rack. Wrap silver-plated wire around the stems where they cross the rack. **16** Screw or nail the rack to a wall using the loops at the base of each hook. If needed, additional nails can be put in each of the corner loops. **17** The wire flowers can be hung individually to a suitable surface by fixing a wire loop to the back of the stem, if desired.

Good illumination is essential during the day for all household and work-related tasks to be carried out safely and effectively. But dim lighting in the evening creates a more relaxed atmosphere, which can be achieved successfully with wall lights, freestanding lamps, and candles. Their soft, diffused light creates exactly the right ambience for unwinding at the end of the day. Floor lamps are ideally suited for lounging on the floor with a good book, lost in a mound

of cushions. Table lamps can be strategically placed around the room, their shades customized to complement the overall decor. Decorate them with a cutwork design, beaded wire, or a stamped pattern. Candles are extremely versatile. Create lanterns with glass containers embellished with twisted wire, which can stand or hang and display the candles safely.

lighting

japanese lamp

The simple lines of Japanese furnishings were the inspiration for this project. The frame is not completely square, but slopes out gently to give a more balanced appearance. The paper used to cover the frame is a traditional paper from Japan called shoji. It has a wonderful soft texture generally used for calligraphy.

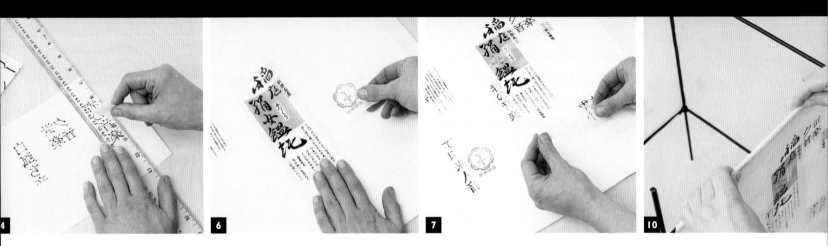

1 The rods need to be welded together. Ask a local welding contractor to build the frame with 4 in. legs and 12 in. between the top and bottom bars. The shorter bars go around the top so that the frame is wider at the base. It is possible to substitute brass rods for the mild steel rods, which can be soldered together. **2** Spray the frame with black paint. **3** Enlarge Japanese text on a photocopier until the symbols are ½ in. high. You can use the sample on page 239. Put the text under the shoji paper and trace directly onto the paper, drawing groups of symbols in a vertical line or square formation. You will need five to seven groups for each panel of the lamp. **4** Hold a ruler on the reverse of the paper and tear down the sides of each group of symbols to make square or rectangular panels. Tear carefully to leave a fluffy edge. **5** Draw a template for the panels of the lampshade. Lay a sheet of shoji paper on top. **6** Cut the noodle wrappers into sections and arrange them within the lines of the template. Tuck the hand-drawn text underneath the noodle wrapping. Once you are happy with the layout, remove the pieces and spray with adhesive, then stick them down in the same arrangement. **7** Tear pieces of handmade Japanese paper and stick, overlapping the text and noodle wrapping. Stick pieces of white tissue paper down in the same way to create areas with several layers of paper. **8** Trim the shoji paper, allowing an extra ¼ in. down each side and ½ in. at the top and bottom. **9** Cut thin strips of double-sided tape to fit along the four bars of the first side of the frame. Position the shoji paper and press onto the frame. **10** Trim diagonally across the corners and stick the allowance to the inside along the top and bottom edges. **11** Continue sticking the side panels to the lamp one at a time. Stick thin strips of double-sided tape down the side edges of the paper before attaching to the frame. **12** Glue the MDF panel to the base to support the light fitting.

materials

¼ in. diameter mild steel rods, four of each length of 22 in., 12½ in., and 12 in.
Sheets of 24 x 17 in. Japanese shoji paper
4 x 12½ in. panel of ⅛ in. MDF
Handmade Japanese paper
White tissue paper
Noodle wrappers
Japanese text
Matte black spray paint
Black ink pen
Ruler
Paper
Scissors
Spray adhesive
Double-sided tape
All-purpose glue

beaded lampshade

Frosted beads on wire, coiled to make a lampshade, catch the light even when the lamp is off. When turned on, the shade positively sparkles! A slim conical shape on a simple curvy metal lampstand has an elegant 1950s look and brings a sculptural element to the room.

materials

Slim terra-cotta pot or shape over which to make the beaded shade
Beads
Small lamp carrier
Medium-grade galvanized garden wire
Fine florist's wire
Blue tack
Jewelry pliers and snippers

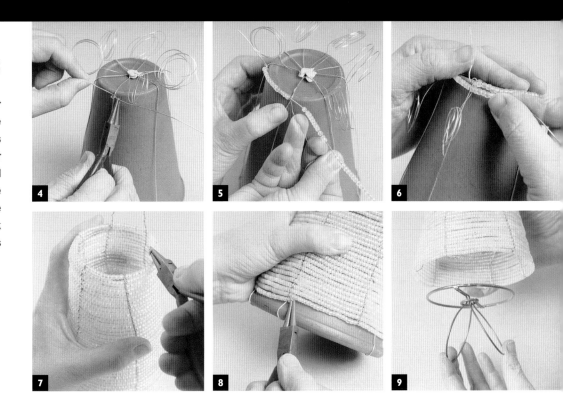

1 Cut three lengths of galvanized wire long enough to run up one side of the shade, over the top, and down the other side, with a little extra at both ends. Space these evenly around the pot to form six struts. **2** Cut six long strands of fine florist's wire, curl the ends, then hold in position with blue tack on top of the pot. **3** Thread a long coil of galvanized wire with the beads of your choice. Do not cut the end of the wire. **4** Using the jewelry pliers, fix the free end of the wire onto a strut at the top of the lampshade. **5** Carefully push the beads up along the wire, then bind the beaded wire firmly in place at the next strut with the florist's wire. **6** Continue winding the beaded wire around the form and bind it in place until the shape is complete. **7** At the end, snip off the wire and use the pliers to make a small loop to secure. **8** Remove the beaded shade from the base. At the top and bottom, neatly fold in the top and bottom struts with pliers. **9** Place the lamp carrier into the lampshade and wire into position using the florist's wire.

accordion wall light

Wall lights cast a soft light on the walls. They are ideal for dining rooms as they allow you to have candles on the table but still give off enough light to allow you to see your meal. The gold leaf and yellow ocher stencil motifs on the unusual tobacco paper produces an attractive wall decoration.

  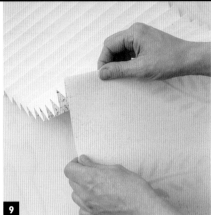 

1 Photocopy or trace the leaf template on page 239. Tape to the cutting mat and secure the stencil film over the top, then cut out along the lines with the craft knife. **2** Cut the tobacco paper and parchment in half lengthwise. Lay the tobacco paper on a flat surface. Using an almost-dry brush, stencil the motif onto the paper. Move the stencil and repeat until there are leaf sprigs scattered all over the paper. **3** Clean and dry the stencil. Reposition it, overlapping one of the leaf motifs. Brush the glue carefully over the stencil film and lift off. **4** Cut a sheet of gold leaf in half. Lay it carefully over the motif and press down carefully with a soft, dry brush. If needed, tear off excess gold leaf to patch other areas of the motif. **5** Allow to dry for a few minutes and then brush lightly with a soft brush to remove the excess gold leaf. Keep the scraps in a container to use at a later date. Complete all the leaf motifs in the same way. **6** Lay the paper face up on several layers of newspaper. Using a piece of sponge, wipe the shellac over the entire surface and allow to dry. This will keep the gold leaf from tarnishing. Dispose of the sponge carefully. **7** Spray adhesive over the parchment and on the back of the tobacco paper and stick together. Smooth the papers together with your hands or a roller to remove any air bubbles. **8** Trim the long sides of the panel to measure 12 in. wide. On the back, mark every 1 in. Use a blunt tool to score between the marks on the back side only. **9** Fold the paper along the score lines to form an accordion. With the right side facing up, trim the panel so that the last fold at each end is a larger "mountain" fold, with the cut edge flat on the table. **10** Punch a small hole through the middle of each panel of the accordion, 1 in. in from each long edge. **11** Thread a length of leather thong through the holes top and bottom. Lift the accordion onto the light fitting and secure the paper to the back side with white gummed tape. Pull the leather thong taut and tape securely. Fit a bulb as recommended by the manufacturer. **12** Replace the light switch cord (if there is one) with leather thong and attach a large gold metal bead to the end.

materials

Semicircular wall light fitting
Tobacco paper
Parchment
"Dutch" gold leaf
Gold bead
Yellow ocher stencil paint
Stencil brush
Stencil film
Craft knife and cutting mat
White school glue
Shellac
Small piece of sponge
Spray adhesive
Masking tape
Paintbrushes
Hole punch
Fine tanned leather thong
White gummed tape

parchment shade

Parchment paper is ideal for the delicate cutwork needed for this project because its stiffness allows the shade to be self-supporting between the two lampshade rings with no ugly uprights to spoil the effect. The mellow shades of parchment paper and natural raffia work well together.

materials

Coolie lampshade
Natural parchment
Lightweight white paper
Natural raffia
Craft knife and cutting mat
All-purpose glue
Double-sided tape
Tapestry needle
Black pen
Pencil
Scissors

1 Open out the old lampshade to draw a template on the white paper. Cut out and fold the template in half three times to make eight equal sections. **2** Open out and fold the last section only in half three times to subdivide it into eight. Mark down the fold lines every ½ in. with a pencil and join the dots to make curved guidelines. **3** Mark *V* shapes with the pen down the third, fifth, and seventh fold lines using the pencil lines to keep the *V*s straight. **4** Cut the parchment lampshade out using the template. **5** Place the template on a cutting mat and position the parchment on top. Cut the *V* shapes straight through the template. Open out each *V* shape with the end of the craft knife. Move the next section of the parchment around and cut another batch of *V* shapes. **6** Continue in this way until each of the eight sections of the parchment has a band of *V* shapes. If desired, cut a circle of *V* shapes in between each band. **7** Overlap the back seam of the parchment, using double-sided tape to stick. **8** Spread a thin layer of glue around the rings of the lampshade and allow to dry until tacky. Fit the top ring first and then lower the shade onto the base ring. **9** Allow to dry, then oversew around the top and bottom edges using natural raffia. Sew in the ends neatly.

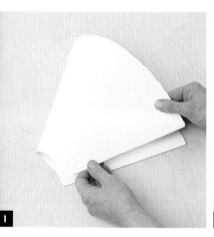

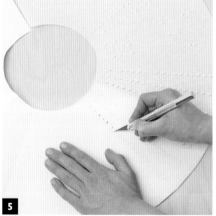
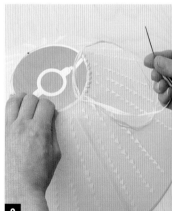

glass jar lanterns

Everyday materials such as glass jars look really stunning decorated with twisted galvanized wire and holding a flickering candle inside. The simple design makes the lanterns suitable for use both indoors and out. Traditional outward-turned scrolls have been used to make the decorative join at the handle tops.

   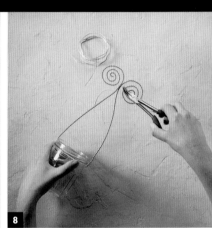

1 Cut two lengths of 16 gauge wire, each 4 ft. long. **2** Cut the sponge in half and place one piece at opposite sides of the glass jar to protect the glass. Place the glass jar and sponges in the vise. **3** Wrap one length of wire around the rim of the jar and twist clockwise to hold in place. **4** Feed the ends of the wire into the chuck of the drill. Tighten to secure, then wind the drill to twist the wire to the required tension. Pull the wire to keep it taut and hold it horizontal. **5** Release the wire from the chuck, then trim the ends. **6** Turn the jar 180° in the vise, then wrap and twist the second length of wire onto the rim in the same way. Trim the wires to the same length. **7** Use the pliers to bend the wire ends into outward-facing spirals, pulling the wire against your thumb to produce a smooth curve. **8** Bind the spirals together three times with the 18 gauge wire. Twist at the back and trim the excess.

materials

Roll of 18 gauge (0.04 in.) galvanized wire
Roll of 16 gauge (0.05 in.) galvanized wire
Wire cutters
Bent-nose pliers
Glass jar
Hand drill
Vise
Small sponge
Scissors

string-stamped lampshade

This textured lampshade has been enhanced by stamping a repeating spiral design in a rich yellow ocher around the base. Try experimenting with pattern, color, and texture, but keep in mind the silhouette effect on your design when the lamp is switched on.

 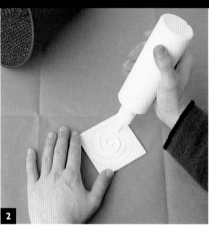 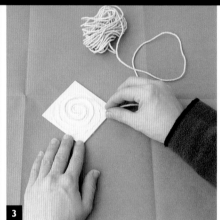 

materials

Burgundy colored, medium-sized
lampshade
Sample pot of yellow ocher acrylic
paint
Cardboard
Glue
Pencil
String
Small roller

1 Copy the scroll template on page 238 onto a small square of cardboard. **2** Pipe glue over the pencil guideline. **3** Starting in the center, curl a length of string around the glue scroll, pressing the string into the glue as you work. Cut off the excess. Allow the stamp to dry. **4** Using a small roller, apply yellow ocher paint to the stamp. **5** Carefully stamp onto the lower edge of the lampshade. Repeat until the border detail is complete. Leave to dry.

woven cane lamp

The hexagonal weave of the cane lamp casts interesting shadows on the table and against the wall when the lamp is lit. Flat band cane is cut from rattan and is easy to work with, as it requires a minimum amount of soaking to make it pliable. The cane can be left in its natural state or stained with a wood dye.

materials

Seventeen lengths of ½ in. flat band cane each 46 in. long
Thirteen lengths of ½ in. flat band cane each 28¼ in. long
2 yd. of ½ in. handle cane
8 in. diameter lampshade ring
Black wood stain
Wood stain thinner
16½ x 12 in. sheet of Japanese paper,
Twelve spring-loaded clothespins
Light fitting and low-energy lightbulb
Hacksaw
Scissors
Large plastic bag

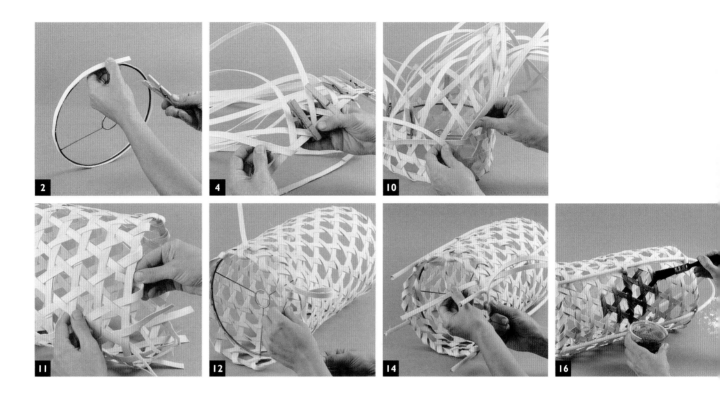

1 Dip the canes in water and put into the plastic bag to keep them damp. Spray them frequently. **2** Bend one of the short lengths around the lampshade ring. Lift off and use a clothespin to hold the overlap. **3** Find the center of a long piece of cane and bend it over the cane ring, with the rough side facing inward. Open the cane to make a sixty degree angle and pin in place. **4** Repeat with the other long pieces. Weave each new piece under the previous one to make a triangle above the cane ring. **5** Pin each triangle and adjust the spacing so that each of the thirteen pieces are the same distance apart. Weave the first and last pieces together to complete the circle. **6** Position the lampshade ring about 1½ in. above the cane ring and pin in place. **7** Take the next short length and fix it with a clothespin, level with the lampshade ring. Weave the length of cane in and out of two of the overlapping uprights to make a triangle. **8** Continue weaving the short length around the lamp's circumference, level with the lampshade ring. Thread the cane under one upright and over the next, and then interlock the two ends above the horizontal ring to produce a series of triangles above the band and a row of hexagonal spaces below it. **9** Overlap the ends of the cane ring and pin together. Adjust the overlap until the cane ring fits snugly around the lampshade ring. Move this ring up 1½ in. and pin in place. **10** Continue adding horizontal strips,

moving the ring each time. Check that the sides are straight and the hexagonal shapes are well formed and of even size. When the lamp is about 15 in. high, unpin the metal ring and dampen the ends of the cane. **11** To make the folded edge, open out each pair of ends in turn and tuck the front end down to the left in front of its partner. Weave underneath the rows below to secure. Fold the back piece forward and to the right, and tuck under the second row. Trim off all ends neatly. **12** Turn the lamp upside down so that the ring you began with is at the top. Secure the ring by wrapping a long piece of cane around it along its length, and tuck the ends into the weave before trimming. **13** Dampen the handle cane and cut in half. Bend the pieces to make an 8 in. diameter curve in the middle to fit the diameter of the lamp. Hold the handle in position and use a length of cane to lash around the top edge (the row you started with) catching in the handle as you go. **14** Using another length of cane, lash around the lampshade along the base and halfway down its length to hold the handle securely. **15** Measure the length of the "legs" (about 4 in.) and saw off the excess cane. **16** Mix a little black wood stain with thinner. Brush over the lamp and leave to dry. **17** Cut the paper in half. Form one half into a loose tube and fit inside the lamp above the ring. Turn upside down and fit the other half in the bottom section. Insert the light fitting and bulb.

momigami lamp

With the ubiquitous Akari lamp by Isamu Noguchi as its inspiration, this paper lamp is made from Penambang cane and Momigami paper. Penambang is a thin, very pliable cane that can be bent into shape while dry. The lamp can be wired with miniature halogen lights, or fitted with tea lights as shown.

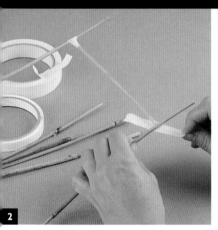

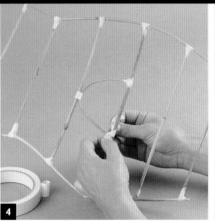

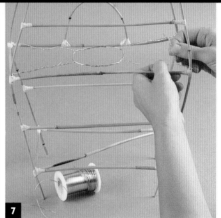

1 Cut four 48 in. lengths of the thinnest, most pliable cane for the curved edges of the lamp. Cut the graded cross struts from straight, strong sections. Cut six 10¼ in. long pieces, twelve 8½ in. pieces, and eight 7¼ in. pieces. **2** Begin with a short cross strut and position it 2 in. from the end of one of the long lengths of cane. Use double-sided tape to secure it and then cover the join with a thin strip of masking tape. **3** Join the other end to another of the long pieces of cane in the same way. Tape the next size of cross strut about 2¾ in. further down the lamp. Continue adding the cross struts in order: short, medium, long, medium, short, and so on, until the three "bumps" of the lamp have been created. **4** Make the back of the lamp to match. Cut three pieces of thin, pliable cane to make portholes for the tea lights—tape the center of the cane to the center of the longest cross strut, then bend the ends to make an arch and tape to the next cross strut. **5** Cut fourteen 4½ in. side struts. Tape these to every second cross strut using thin strips of masking tape. Then trim the "legs" at each end of the lamp. **6** Cut and fit single diagonal struts inside the lamp to strengthen the structure. Fit crossed diagonal struts at the top to allow you to hang

it up (if required). **7** Make a coil of wire to fit around a glass tea light holder. Wrap wire around the length of the coil to strengthen it. Attach the ring in the center of the lamp's frame behind one of the archways with a length of wire to each corner. Do this for each of the three lights. **8** Cut a piece of Momigami paper slightly larger than the front of the framework. Dilute the craft glue with five parts water. Use a brush or sponge to apply the glue to one side of the paper. Lay the pasted paper over the framework and press down gently along the edges. Allow to dry. **9** Turn the frame over and stick a piece of Momigami paper to the reverse side. Once the paper has dried, cut around the inside of the archways, leaving a ¼ in. seam allowance. Glue the cut edges inside the frames of the archways. **10** Tear or cut the excess paper down the sides of the framework. Cut the top and bottom edges with a ¼ in. seam allowance and glue neatly inside. **11** Stand the frame on its side and apply paper to the sides of the lamp in the same way. Allow the paper to dry before moving the lamp. **12** Tear or cut off the excess paper and paste down any ragged edges to complete the lamp. Spray the lamp inside and out with fire-retardant spray.

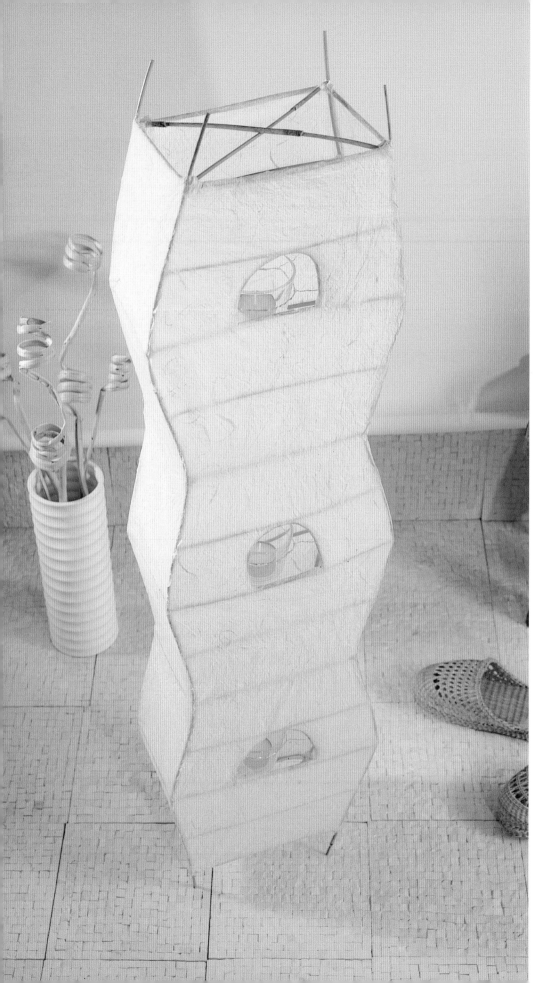

materials

16 oz. of ¼ in. Penambang cane
Natural colored Momigami paper
3 yd. of 24 gauge (0.02 in.) silver-
plated wire
Three tea lights
Double-sided tape, ¼ in. wide
Lightweight masking tape
Wire cutters
White craft glue
Small brush or sponge
Scissors
Fire-retardant spray

It is the personal items that make a home—the family snapshots displayed in photograph frames and albums, the letters from friends stored neatly in a letter holder. A living space is further enhanced by the individual touches—a couple of bobbing hydrangea heads or dried stems in a stunning vase, exquisite bowls arranged decoratively on a tabletop. This chapter includes projects to protect and exhibit your treasured possessions as well as objects

you can make to add points of interest to a room. Choose from a picture frame wrapped with paper string and a wire ring holder over which to hook rings and drape necklaces and charm bracelets, to a hammered mirror frame or beaded wire picture frame, and miniature molded soap blocks to place next to the sink in the guest bathroom.

display

beaded candlestick

The design and construction of this candlestick is influenced by the shape and form of a metal tart pan. The wire frame is molded into the base of the tiny tart pan, the fluted sides holding the wire evenly in place. When lit, the candle flame reflects in each facet of the colored glass beads.

1 Cut eight lengths of wire 10½ in. long. **2** Place each wire over a solid metal base and flatten approximately 1½ in. in the middle by hitting hard with the flat side of the head of a hammer. **3** Using the pliers, bend up each side of the flattened center. **4** Place each wire into the base of the case, overlaying the wires and pushing each side into opposite grooves on the case sides. Hold the wires temporarily in place with a small piece of blue tack. Repeat steps 1–4 for all the grooves in the case. **5** Mix up a quantity of the resin glue and coat the base and the wires with it. Allow it to set before removing the blue tack. **6** Using wire cutters, trim the excess wire. **7** Thread six beads onto each wire, then use the pliers to form a small loop in the top of each wire. **8** With your hands, curve the wires to form a tulip shape.

materials

0.06 in. thick tinned copper wire
3 in. diameter tin tart pan
Faceted glass beads in shades of
pink, red, purple, and blue
Resin glue
Spatula
Bent-nose pliers
Wire cutters
Two hammers
Blue tack

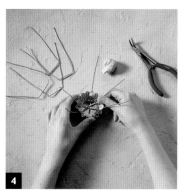

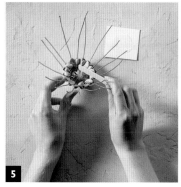

stained-glass vase

The challenge in making this vase is keeping the pattern subtle so as not to overpower the flowers it displays, yet keeping it interesting enough to stand as a beautiful object in its own right. Visit a stained-glass artist or workshop to find offcuts of a wide range of colored and textured glass.

2

3

6

8

materials

**Large glass vase, approximately
16 x 6½ in.
Stained-glass scraps in blues and
greens
Permanent marker
Glass cutter
Protective goggles
Contact adhesive
Small narrow paintbrush
Waterproof grout
Spatula
Squeegee
Sponge
Stainless-steel scourer
Clear floor wax**

1 Enlarge the template on page 240 on a photocopier to fit around the inside of the vase. **2** With the lines facing out, draw over the pattern on the outside of the glass with the permanent marker. Remove the paper template. **3** Choose one shade of glass for the main lines in the drawing. Score the pieces into strips (approximately ¼ in. wide) and tap along the back of each score line with the ball end of the glass cutter. **4** Score the strips into small rectangles, ½–¾ in. long and tap these off. **5** With the paintbrush, paint contact adhesive over the main lines on the vase and leave to set. Working with a number of pieces at a time, paint one side of each piece of cut glass with a thin coat of contact adhesive and leave to set. **6** Press the glass in place over the lines, following the pattern and keeping the pieces close together. **7** Continue working the pattern outward. Surround each mosaic line with a different color of glass, and then work a "background" of patches of different shades of blues and greens to fill in all the spaces. Leave to set for twenty-four hours. **8** Spread grout over the surface of the stained glass with a spatula, filling in all of the gaps. Using the squeegee, scrape off as much grout as you can. **9** Working next to running water, soak and wring out the sponge, and wipe down the vase, removing as much excess grout as you can. It will not all come off at this stage. Smooth out the top and bottom edges of the vase with some grout and a damp sponge. Leave to set for twelve to twenty-four hours. **10** With the scourer, gently rub the mosaic to remove any residue grout. Use a damp sponge to remove any grout dust. **11** Rub on a light coat of the wax and leave to dry.

photograph album

The delightful quality of this album is that it can be opened out like an accordion, with the pages laid out flat or flipped over for viewing. Methyl cellulose has been used here as a sizing medium to stiffen the boards and cloth and keep them from warping as you make the album.

materials

24 x 18 in. sheet display board
18 x 51 in. crushed suede
12 in. square white cotton chintz
Three 23 x 8 in. sheets of artist's
rag/handmade paper
2 oz. copper seed beads
2 oz. gold tube beads
Colored thread to match the beads
Two 11½ x 8½ in. sheets of
decorative endpapers
Methyl cellulose
White school glue
Soft-bristle glue brush
Pencils
Ruler
Artist's scalpel or knife
Circle stencil ½ in. diameter
Beading needle
Scissors
Chalk pencil
Newspaper
Waxed paper
Heavy books
Bone folder or ruler

1 Cut two cover boards 8½ x 12 in. from the display board, and two pieces of suede 10½ x 13½ in. From the chintz cut two pieces 8¼ x 1 in. and two pieces 8¼ x ½ in. **2** To make a sizing medium, mix 2 oz. methyl cellulose with 4 fl. oz. cold water until smooth. Stir in an equal amount of white school glue and mix thoroughly. **3** Place the cover boards on newspaper and with the glue brush paint a thin layer of sizing medium over each. Keep the brush strokes in the same direction. Leave to dry. **4** Paint a second coat with brush strokes in the opposite direction and leave to dry. Turn the boards over and repeat. **5** Place the crushed suede face down on clean newspaper and paint with a thin coat of sizing medium. Leave to dry. Repeat with the chintz strips. **6** Fold all the paper sheets in half using a bone folder to get a flat, crisp edge. **7** To make the accordion pages for the album, take one ½ in. strip of chintz and paint the sized side with a thin layer of glue. Align the edges of two sheets of paper along the center of the strip (folded hills of the sheets facing up), and press firmly into place. **8** Paint a thin layer of glue on the second piece of chintz and attach the third sheet of folded paper to the second in the same way. Allow to dry flat. **9** Fold the pages along the joints and folds into a neat, flat accordion. **10** Place both pieces of suede right side down on a hard surface. Place a cover board in the middle of each, ensure that all edges are even, and trace around the board with the chalk pencil. Put the piece for the back and the boards aside. **11** Working along the chalk lines on the front piece, lightly mark a point with the chalk pencil 1 in. in from the corner of each long side. Then mark every 1½ in. in between the two points. Mark points at similar intervals along both short sides. **12** Line up the dots and mark every 1½ in. across and down the material to give you seven rows across the album and five rows down. **13** In pencil, mark the

top-left corner dot with an X, then mark every other dot, row by row down the album. **14** Center a circle stencil of ½ in. diameter over each remaining dot and draw a circle with a sharpened pencil. When you turn the fabric over, there should now be a distinct impression of Os and Xs. **15** Thread a beading needle with thread to match the color of the beads and sew approximately fifteen seed beads over the circle outlines with a backstitch. **16** Sew four tube beads over the Xs. **17** Lay both pieces of suede right side down on clean newspaper. Brush a thin coat of glue across the back of one piece, lay a cover board inside the chalk lines, turn it over, and with a bone folder gently smooth out the air bubbles. **18** Turn it face down again, touching up the glue if necessary. Trim the corners of the cloth to ½ in. from the corner of the board. Fold the top and bottom edges onto the board, smoothing firmly into place. **19** Before folding in the side edges, tuck the corners in, hospital-bed style. Fold over the sides and press into place. Repeat with the other cloth cover. Leave to dry. **20** Brush about ¼ in. in along one edge of the 1 in. wide chintz with white school glue. With the paper accordion in front of you with the chintz edges to the left and folded edges to the right, glue the edge of the chintz to the top edge of the back page. **21** Take the other strip, brush with glue in the same way, and stick to the back edge of the top page. Leave to dry. **22** Use a bone folder to fold the extra chintz over, paint the back with glue, and attach to the cover boards one at a time. Leave to dry. **23** Adjust the size of the end papers if necessary and brush with glue. Stick in the center of the boards over the chintz with a ⅛ in. border of suede showing. Press out all air bubbles with a bone folder. **24** Place a piece of waxed paper between the cover board and pages, and press the album under heavy books overnight.

handmade paper notebooks

There are many occasions when you might want to record something in a special book. Here the leaves have been bonded between two layers of fusible web that adheres the leaves to the surface and provides a protective layer on top.

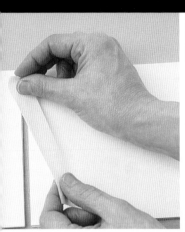

1 Cut four pieces of cardboard 6 x 9 in. and trim off a 1¼ in. wide strip from one end of each. Set these strips aside. 2 Stick two boards together to make up a double thickness for the front, and again for the back. 3 Place the strips parallel with the main panels, ¼ in. away, and stick together with gummed tape. Turn the panels over and repeat. 4 Cut the tissue paper ½ in. larger than the cover panels. Spray adhesive on one side, center the tissue paper over the panels and stick in place. Miter the corners and stick the overlap to the reverse side. 5 Place the mottled paper over the front panel and crease to mark the edges of the cover. Cut a piece of fusible web to fit just inside the creases. Iron in position. Peel off the backing paper. Arrange the leaves on top. 6 Place a sheet of web on top and press. Allow to cool before peeling off the backing paper. 7 Spray the reverse of the mottled paper with adhesive. Place the paper over the front cover, lining the creases up with the edge of the panel. Smooth out toward the edges to stick, and trim ¾ in. larger than the panel. 8 Turn the panel over and fold in the overlap, mitering the corners. 9 Cut a piece of mottled paper to fit ¼ in. in from the edges. Stick on the inside of the cover. Cover the back of the notebook in the same way without the leaves. 10 Mark the position of the holes in the middle of the end strips. Punch through the cardboard with a bradawl. 11 Cut pieces of watercolor paper to fit inside the covers. Mark the position of the holes and punch two or three sheets at a time. 12 Thread hemp through the holes in the back cover and add the sheets of paper. Thread the string through and tie in a bow.

materials

Mat board or thick cardboard
White tissue paper
Mottled handmade paper
Watercolor paper
Pressed leaves
Fusible web
Hemp string
Spray adhesive
Hole punch
Craft knife and cutting mat
Bradawl or similar tool
Ruler
Gummed tape
Iron

stenciled letter holder

A blank letter rack has been painted and stenciled, then distressed with aging techniques. Crackle varnish is applied to the dry surface and then dried with a hair dryer. The distressed effect is achieved by rubbing burnt sienna oil paint over the crackled surface.

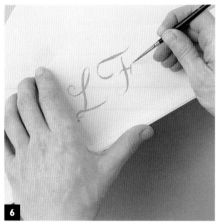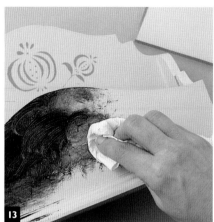

1 Remove the center panel of the letter rack for ease of handling, then apply two coats of mint-green paint. Avoid painting the edges of the middle panel that fit into the side grooves. Sand lightly when completely dry. **2** Enlarge the initials template on page 240 on a photocopier to an appropriate size and draw over the outlines with a black pen. **3** Trace the pomegranates on page 240 and outline with a black pen. Place the tracings on a cutting mat and tape a piece of stencil paper on top of each. Using the craft knife, cut out the larger shapes. The fine lines on the letters and tiny details such as the stems and dots on the small pomegranates can be added later by hand. **4** Apply spray adhesive to the reverse of the stencils and allow to dry. Position the letter stencil in the middle of the front panel and press firmly to stick. **5** Apply the gold paint carefully, building up the depth of color slowly to keep the paint from seeping under the stencil. **6** Peel off the stencil and complete the letters in pencil. Use a very fine brush to go over the lines with gold paint. **7** Stick the pomegranate stencils on the back panel of the letter rack in the same way and apply the gold paint as before. Peel off the stencils and add the fine details with a paintbrush. **8** Stencil a small pomegranate on each side of the initials. Leave the stems unpainted but paint in the other fine details. **9** Paint the front surface of the middle panel first and then the letter holder with an even coat of ageing varnish. **10** Leave the varnish for about 1½–2 hours until it is almost dry. The timing depends on the temperature and humidity of the room. The varnish will dry more quickly in a warmer, drier atmosphere. **11** Paint the middle panel of the letter rack with crackle varnish. Use your finger to gently smooth the surface. This removes the brush marks, ensuring that the varnish is absolutely flat and that no areas have been missed. **12** Dry the panel with a hair dryer held 8–12 in. away. Stop once the cracks begin to form. If you are satisfied with the cracking, apply the crackle varnish to the letter rack in the same way and dry with the hair dryer. If the cracking is unsatisfactory wash off the varnish and repeat, allowing the varnish more time to dry. Leave to dry overnight. **13** Use a paper towel to rub oil paint over the whole surface. Wipe off the excess and buff with a soft cloth, leaving the dark oil paint showing in the cracks. **14** Insert the middle panel. Dip your finger in wax gilt and wipe along the bottom rim and top edges of the rack. Paint all surfaces with two coats of matte polyurethane varnish. Cut a piece of felt to fit the bottom of the rack and glue in position to finish.

materials

Blank letter rack
Mint-green flat paint
Stencil paper
Gold stencil paint
Stencil brush
Two-step crackle varnish
Burnt sienna oil paint
Scraps of felt
Spray adhesive
Wax gilt
Matte polyurethane varnish
Craft knife and cutting mat
Fine-grade sandpaper
Black pen
Masking tape
Paintbrushes
All-purpose glue
Hair dryer
Kitchen paper towel
Soft cloth

hammered mirror frame

It is often the more prosaic materials that prove to be the most interesting when applied in a new way. This mirror frame has been covered with roofing flashing, then beaten to give a hammered effect. As flashing comes in strips of no more than 16 in., it works best when used on small sections.

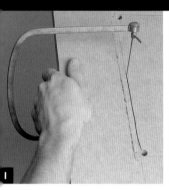
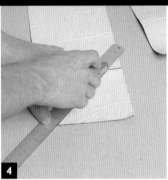

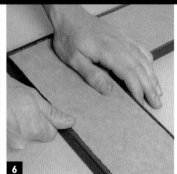

materials

18 in. square MDF
6 in. wide roofing flashing
12 in. square mirrored glass
Four mirror corners and screws
Keyhole hanger and screws
Washers for spacers
Jigsaw or fretsaw
Steel rule
Craft knife
Waterproofed cloth tape
Ball-headed hammer
Pen or pencil
Screwdriver
Cardboard

1 From the MDF, cut out a 4 in. frame. **2** Cut four pieces of flashing 18 in. long. Measure 1 in. in from each long edge and draw a line along the length. These are the fold lines. **3** Measure 4 in. in from each short end and mark on the fold line. **4** Draw a miter from the marked 4 in. point to the corner at the opposite side. Cut along this line. Repeat at the other end. Make four. **5** Try the pieces against the frame. Peel off the backing and stick each in place. **6** Fold the 1 in. edges in and stick to the back of the frame. **7** Using the cloth tape, cover the turned-over edges of the roofing flashing. **8** Turn to the front of the frame. Using a ball-headed hammer, cover the whole surface of the roofing flashing with a random pattern of indentations. **9** Screw the mirror glass in place using mirror corners. Pack with cardboard to ensure a snug fit. **10** Screw a keyhole hanger to the center of the back of the frame. Use washers as spacers to bring the hanger level with the back surface of the glass.

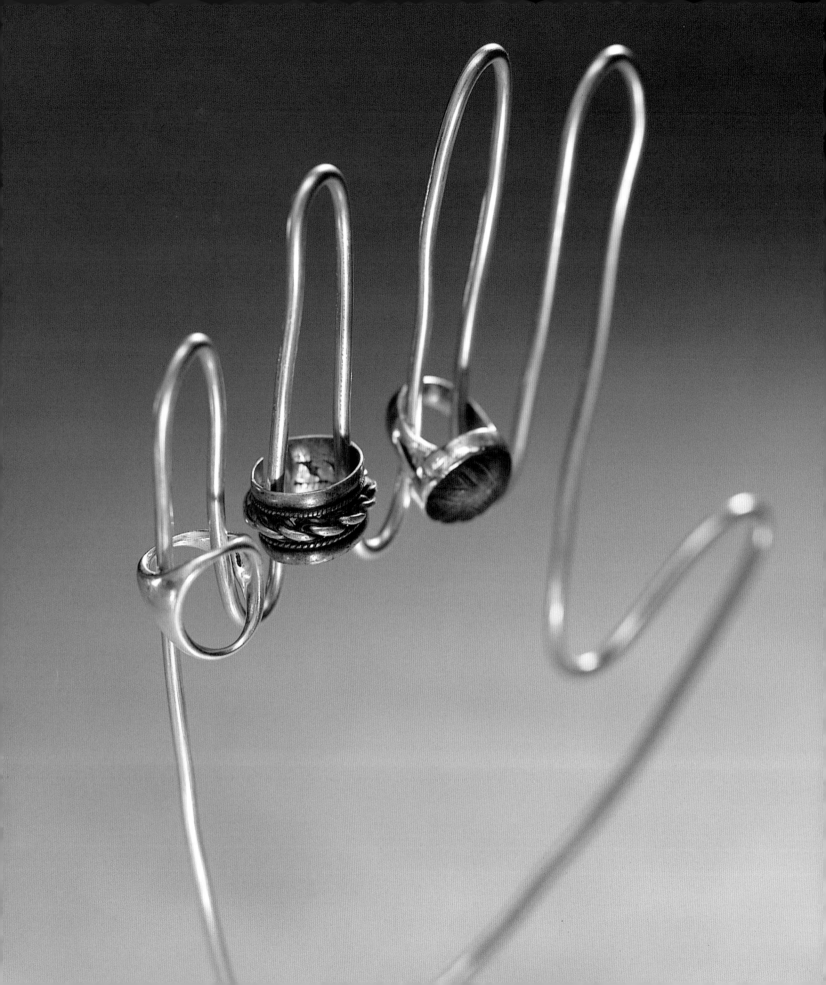

hand ring holder

Soft aluminum wire is satisfyingly pliable and although it is relatively thick, it is easy to bend into smooth curves. The challenge is in manipulating the shape from just one continuous length of wire. The form of the hand is a logical choice for a ring holder, but it is also ideal for hanging earrings.

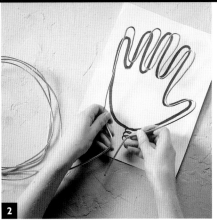

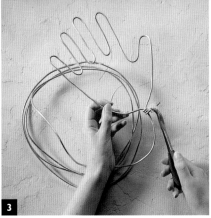

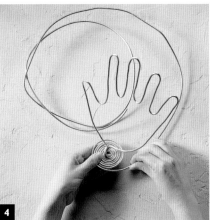

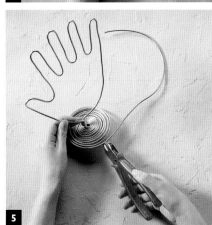

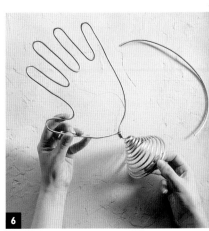

materials

3¼ yd. of 0.12 in. thick aluminum wire
Wire cutters
Bent-nose pliers
Small sheet of paper

1 Trace or photocopy the template on page 241. Leaving a 4 in. end of wire at the base of the palm, carefully bend the wire around the thumb and fingers. **2** Continue bending the wire around the hand and make a right-angled turn when you come to the wrist. **3** Twist the 4 in. length of wire very tightly, three times around the remaining longer section of wire using pliers. Trim the excess from the short length only, at the back of the hand. When twisting the

wires together, to protect the surface of the aluminum, put a small piece of paper between the wire and the pliers. **4** Bind the remaining longer wire length into a tight, flat coil, forming smooth curves with your thumb and forefinger. **5** Bind the coil eleven times. Trim the excess at the back of the hand. **6** Pull the coil so that it opens slightly and stands upright—the tighter coils are much more difficult to manipulate.

tall vases

The shape of these vases is built from five simple pieces of cardboard taped together. This is covered with an attractive crinkled paper ribbon and painted. Paper ribbon is sold in flower shops and greeting-card stores. Sometimes it is sold twisted into a thick rope that needs to be unraveled before use.

   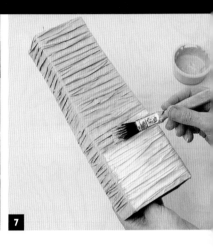

materials

Corrugated cardboard
Paper ribbon
Acrylic paint
Paintbrush
Spray acrylic glaze
Silver sand
White school glue
Craft knife and cutting mat
Brown gummed tape
Scissors
Pencil

1 Enlarge the template on page 242 and cut out. Use it to cut two pieces of corrugated cardboard. Cut two strips for the sides of the vase measuring 11 x 1¾ in. and a piece to fit across the base of the vase. **2** Stick the pieces of corrugated cardboard together with strips of brown gummed tape. Make sure that the bottom of the vase is level before attaching the base piece. **3** Open out the paper ribbon and cut in half lengthwise. Cut each half in two again to make four long, narrow strips of crinkled paper. **4** Starting from the base, cover part of the vase with white school glue and wrap ribbon strips around it, overlapping as you go. Keep the paper quite tight but encourage the natural crinkles on the ribbon to form. **5** Continue pasting the vase and sticking down the ribbon. Add extra lengths as needed. Tuck the end of each ribbon under the previous layer. **6** Allow the edge of the last layer of ribbon to stick up about ½ in. above the vase. Smooth out the top part of the ribbon and snip into each corner. Glue the overlap down onto the inside edge. **7** Paint the vase with two coats of acrylic paint. Allow to dry and spray with a clear acrylic glaze. **8** Fill the vase partway with silver sand to weigh down the bottom.

beaded-wire picture frame

Aluminum and tinned copper wire are soft, so can be twisted easily into looped circles. A number of irregularly shaped, blue and green glass beads have been threaded onto the silvery wire to offset the deep blue of the painted round frame.

materials

Small, round painted picture frame,
6 in. diameter
Approximately thirty-two blue and
green glass beads with holes of
more than 0.04 in.
18 gauge (0.04 in.) aluminum or
tinned copper wire
Round-nose pliers
Wire cutters
Strong white glue

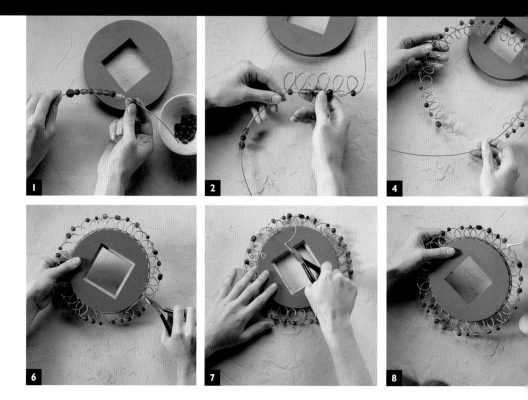

1 Cut a length of wire 2 yd. long. Take care not to bend or twist it at this stage. Thread on the beads. **2** Make small loops from the left by bending the wire carefully, using about 2¼ in. for each loop. Push a single bead into place before each loop. **3** Continue making loops and threading the beads until you have enough to stretch around the frame. **4** Cut another length of wire 31½ in. long and thread through the loops until it makes a complete circle with an equal length of wire sticking out at each end. **5** Fit around the edge of the frame, pull the wire tight, and twist the two ends together first with your fingers. **6** Twist the two ends firmly together with the pliers to make a snug fit. **7** Turn to the back of the frame and open out the two lengths of wire. Twist the ends with the pliers to make the frame stand. **8** Working from the front of the frame, put a dab of glue onto each end of the looped wire, place a bead onto one of the glued ends, and push the other end into the bead to join.

paper picture frames

In this project, basic picture frames have been covered using flat paper yarn in a range of harmonizing colors. Paper yarn is a versatile material that can be coiled, woven, knitted, or even crocheted to produce all sorts of attractive effects that can be created quickly and easily.

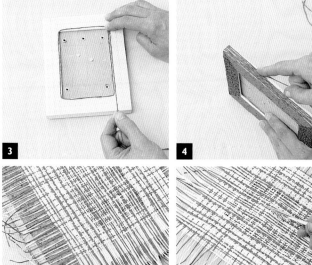

materials

Basic picture frames
Flat paper yarn in colors of
marshmallow, ginger, white,
and spice
White paper
White gummed tape
Double-sided tape
Corkboard
Tapestry needle
Glass-headed pins
Scissors
Paper
Pencil

coiled string frame

1 Cover the front of the frame with double-sided tape, making sure that the tape goes to the edges of the aperture and the frame. **2** Cut two long lengths of ginger flat paper yarn to twist together to form a thicker round string. Tie two cut ends to a door and tie the other ends to a pencil. Hold the paper yarn fairly taut and rotate the pencil with your fingers until the string is tightly twisted. **3** Cut the knots off one end of the paper string and stick it to the inside edge of the frame aperture. Start winding the paper string around the frame aperture and sticking it down. Fold the corners neatly to create the appearance of lines radiating to the corners of the frame. **4** Once the front is covered with string, stick double-sided tape to the edge of the frame, then continue wrapping the string around the frame to cover the sides. **5** Trim the end of the string and tuck the end underneath the previous rows. Press the string firmly in place to secure.

woven frame

6 Make a paper template of the front of the frame. Attach this to the board. Stick double-sided tape about ¾–1¼ in. from the outside edge of the template. **7** Cut lengths of paper yarn to fit lengthwise between the strips of tape (warp threads). Remove the backing from the top and bottom tapes and stick the lengths down, leaving a small gap between each piece. **8** Weave lengths (weft threads) of yarn under and over the warp threads. Once you have woven several weft threads, remove some of the backing paper from the double-sided tape on the sides and stick the paper yarn in place. **9** Continue weaving in the weft threads. Use the tapestry needle to ease the yarn into position. As you work down the frame, insert glass-headed pins to hold the middle of the weft in position and then pull the ends out to straighten. **10** Once the template is covered, ease the weaving off the tape. Follow step 1 of the coiled string frame and stick the woven frame in position. **11** Cut across the weft threads between the warp threads near the edge of the aperture. Cut across the warp threads between the weft threads. **12** Stick a narrow strip of double-sided tape on the inside of the aperture rim. Unravel the weaving inside the aperture and stick the threads on the back side. **13** Stick double-sided tape on the back side of the frame. Wrap the threads around and stick down. Cover the ends with strips of white gummed paper.

lace paper bowls

Papier-mâché is normally done with newspaper, but any type of paper can be used. This exquisite lace paper from Japan is very delicate but becomes stiff when brushed with glue. It comes in a variety of patterns that can be used to great effect to create some unusual and pretty edges to the bowls.

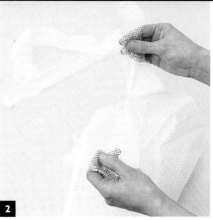
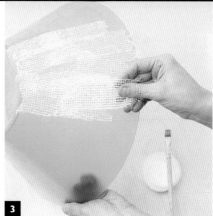

materials

Japanese lace paper—Mizutamashi and Rakusui Usumaki
Pressed flowers, leaves, or feathers
Large plastic bowl
Petroleum jelly
White school glue
Paste brush
Palette knife

1 Smear the outside of the plastic bowl with petroleum jelly. **2** Tear pieces of Japanese paper into strips about 1 in. wide and then into ragged pieces about 3 in. long. Do not use any solid areas in the paper so that the finished bowls will have a light, airy appearance. **3** Dilute the white school glue with five times as much water. Brush the paper strips with the glue and lay onto the bowl, overlapping the edges slightly. **4** Cover the entire bowl with several layers of paper, leaving the top edge very ragged. Leave to dry overnight. **5** Squeeze the plastic bowl to ease the papier-mâché structure off the sides. If necessary you can slip a palette knife gently down between the bowl and the papier-mâché. **6** Remove the plastic bowl and test the strength of the papier-mâché. If necessary, replace the plastic bowl and add one or two more layers of the Japanese paper. **7** With the plastic bowl back in place, decorate the papier-mâché with pressed flowers, leaves, or feathers, if desired. Paste the additions onto the outside of the bowl and then tear pieces of Japanese paper to cover and secure them. Allow to dry completely again before removing the bowl.

mini soap blocks

These citrus soaps are so easy to make. Translucent glycerine soap compound is available from craft suppliers and you can make the finished product more interesting by adding a few drops of your choice of scent or color and appropriate natural materials such as the zest of limes, oranges, and lemons.

materials

Glycerin soap compound, ½ lb. of
each color
Cosmetic colors
Cosmetic scent
Citrus fruits
Zester
Heatproof dish
Double boiler
Grater
Milk carton or similar container
Scissors
Cocktail sticks
Sharp knife

1 Grate the soap compound into a heatproof dish and place in a double boiler over the heat until it melts. If using the microwave, heat on full power and check every ten seconds. Be careful, as the soap melts suddenly and will boil over and may even ignite if heated too long. 2 Remove the dish from the heat. Add a few drops of color as desired. Then add a few drops of scent. Set aside. 3 Cut a carton down to 2 in. high. 4 Using a zester, cut thin strips of peel from a citrus fruit and drop into the base of the carton. 5 Reheat the soap compound if a skin has formed on the surface, then pour the liquid into the carton. 6 Use a cocktail stick to distribute the peel and allow to cool before placing the carton in the refrigerator. 7 Once the soap has set (about one hour), it can be turned out. Ease the sides of the carton away from the soap and press the base of the carton until the soap drops out. Cut into four.

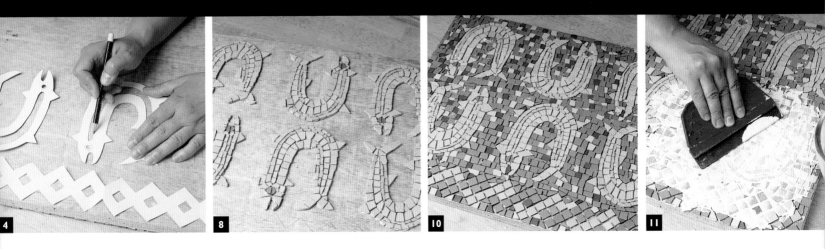

1 If the backsplash is to be secured to a wall, measure, mark, and drill four corners for screw holes in the plywood. **2** Sand the surface and edges of the plywood. Mix two parts glue to one part water and brush this on the front and edges. Leave to dry. **3** Photocopy the templates on page 242. Stick these onto thin cardboard and cut out. **4** Place in position on the plywood with even spacing between and trace around them with a pencil. **5** Soak all the tiles in water for fifteen minutes and peel away their paper backing. Lay them out to dry. **6** Begin tiling the fish by working each one from the inside out. Cut a small quantity of pink tiles into quarters with a pair of tile nippers. Nip each quarter to fit the shape of the pattern. Place them in position, working through all of the pink lines before sticking. **7** "Butter" a small amount of grout/adhesive onto the backs of the tiles with an artist's palette knife and stick them down securely. **8** Do the same with the speckled gray and dark gray tiles to complete the body and add the eye from the green/gray tile. **9** Cut the gray and green/gray tiles for the border into quarters and lay them all out in the pattern before sticking them down. Use the main picture as a reference. Avoid covering the holes drilled in the corners. Leave to dry for a day. **10** To lay the background, cut the four shades of blue tiles into quarters. Begin working the pattern from around the fish outward in a grid pattern, keeping a random color mix. Leave the drilled holes exposed but cut four tiles for their places and keep to one side. Leave to dry for a day. **11** Spread a generous quantity of grout/adhesive over the surface of the mosaic with the grout spreader, filling in all the gaps (except for the drilled holes). With the spreader, scrape off as much excess grout as possible. **12** Using the grout spreader and a damp sponge spread grout around the edges of the plywood and smooth the surface over with a damp sponge. **13** With a clean, damp sponge, wipe the mosaic surface clean. Leave to dry for a day. **14** Wipe the mosaic with a soft cloth to remove any residue. **15** Mark and drill holes in the wall, put in sinkers, and screw the backsplash in place. **16** Use grout to fill in the gaps over the screw heads and stick the tiles for the four holes. Rub a small amount of grout across the surface to fill in any gaps, wipe clean, and leave to dry. **17** Wipe a thin film of clear floor wax over the tiles and around the edges over the grout for shine. Leave to dry.

materials

¾ in. thick sheet of plywood, cut to 16 x 19 in.

4 in. square sheet of 1 in. ceramic mosaic tiles in the following quantities: four salmon-pink, nine speckled gray, three dark gray, one green/gray, four dark blue/green, four pale blue, four blue/gray, two dark blue

Drill and bits
Medium-grade sandpaper
White school glue
Pencil
Thin card
Protective goggles
Tile nippers
Waterproof grout/adhesive
Artist's palette knife

Sponge
Grout spreader
Screws and wall sinkers
Screwdriver
Scissors
Soft cloth
Clear floor wax

Entertaining does not just mean an extravagant dinner party using expensive glassware and china. It can include a light lunch in the sunroom or a last-minute meal organized for friends. There are a range of things you can make for such occasions, from mats and runners to table decorations. At the more extravagant end of the spectrum, projects include beaded fruit to make a centerpiece and a frosted glass bowl that you can use for floating

candles. For more casual meals, there are place mats that are finished with crisp mitered corners to give them a neat appearance; serving spoons, which are created simply by wrapping colored string and beads around the handles of ordinary wooden spoons; and a round platter enhanced with a striking red and white mosaic design for serving cold meats and cheeses.

entertaining

simple place mats

A neat mitered border is all you need to design endless place mat combinations, providing color schemes for every occasion. These place mats are made from an inexpensive, heavy, Indian cotton that comes in a rainbow of colors.

1 For each mat, from the main color cut one piece 17¾ x 14 in. **2** From the contrast color, cut two strips 2¾ x 14 in. and two strips 2¾ x 17¾ in. **3** Turn down one corner of each end of the contrast strips and press with your fingertips to mark the miters. Unfold. **4** Place two strips right sides together, then stitch along the crease line. Repeat with the other three strips, stitching each together to make a "frame." Trim the miters close to the seams. **5** Press the miters open. **6** Pin the contrast frame to the main mat piece, right sides together, along the miter seam. Make sure the miter lies flat. **7** Stitch around the outside edge of the mat. Press seams open and trim. **8** Turn the contrast to the right side. Turn in a hem on the inside of the frame. Slipstitch in place.

materials

FOR SIX MATS
¾ yd. heavy cotton in the main color
½ yd. heavy cotton in the contrast color
Sewing machine
Sewing kit

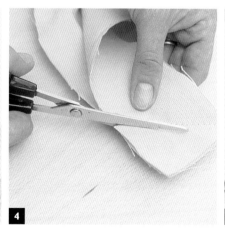

salad bowl

Jazz up a plain wooden salad bowl with a decorative beadwork pattern. Search out a selection of beads in different shapes and sizes, choosing the colors to complement your dinner table. With a hammer and some nails, your next salad will be transformed.

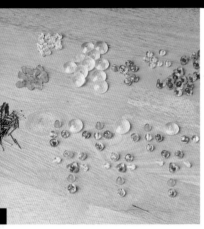

materials

Wooden salad bowl 6 in. tall, 9 in. across the top, with walls ¾ in. thick
Variety of ½ in. long panel pins or wood nails to fit the holes in the beads
Variety of beads:
Seventeen crystal disk beads ¾ in.
26 blue pyramid glass beads ¼ in.
13 orange triangle glass beads ⁵⁄₁₆ in.
26 blue round glass beads ¼ in.
52 orange round glass beads ¼ in.
13 crystal round glass beads ¼ in.
26 crystal faceted glass beads ¼ in.
Hammer
Dressmaker's measuring tape
Soft lead pencil

1 Using a combination of beads of your own choice, lay out the glass beads in a repeat pattern of 8 in. wide to get a good idea of how they will look on the bowl. **2** Choose one bead at the top edge of the pattern and measure the repeat distance between each of the same type. **3** Measure around the top rim of the bowl where that bead will be placed and adjust the distance of the beads if necessary to make the pattern fit evenly around the circumference of the bowl. Remember that the bowl tapers, so the space between the beads at the bottom of the pattern will be closer than at the top. **4** Mark the positions of the first bead in the pattern using the dressmaker's tape and soft lead pencil. **5** Take the total number of first beads in the pattern and nail each one into place on the bowl using the pins or nails. **6** Following the bead pattern laid out before you as a guide and working one type of colored bead at a time all the way around the bowl, nail the remaining beads into place. **7** Turn the bowl over and nail four large, disk-shaped beads onto the bottom, close to the edge and evenly spaced.

serving spoons

If you need a last-minute solution to dressing up a dinner table, this is a quick and easy answer. Open up all those drawers full of odds and ends, pour out your secret stash of buttons, and mix or match them. Then thread them onto decorative twine and wrap them onto the plainest wooden spoons in the house.

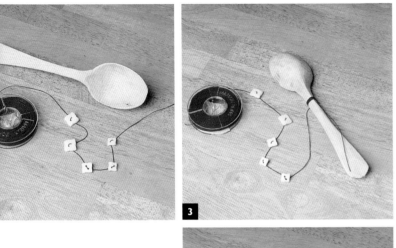

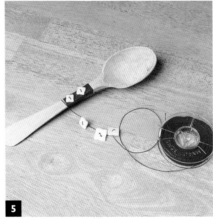

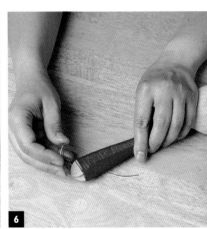

1 Arrange the buttons in the sequence you want them to appear on the spoon, then thread them onto the twine or cord, working from top to bottom at the tail end of the twine. **2** Leaving a tail of 2 in., glue the twine with a thin line of glue down the center back of the spoon 1 in. from the tip of the handle to where you wish to begin wrapping. Leave to dry. **3** Holding the twine in place at the base of the handle, begin wrapping it tightly around the handle. Push down on it as you go to keep the spacing neat. **4** Wrap approximately fifteen times and bring forward the first button. Push it into place on the front center of the handle. Keep the twine tight to hold it in place. **5** Continue wrapping and adding in the buttons with even spacing between each one. Finish wrapping 1 in. from the tip of the handle. **6** Tie a small, tight knot with the two ends of twine. Thread the needle with one end of twine and draw it through the wrapped twine at the back of the handle and out again 1 in. down. Cut off the end and do the same to the other tail end. **7** If the twine or cord that you have used is soft, put a small dab of white school glue on the back side of the knot and glue hidden under the edge of the twine.

materials

Two 8 in. wooden spoons
Four or five mother-of-pearl buttons
in two or three graded sizes
6 yd. colored polyester whipping
twine or silk beading cord
White school glue
Large-eyed half round upholstery
needle

raffia table runner

Raffia bends and flows as easily as any cotton or wool, and holds its shape beautifully. You can wash and iron the runner just as you would any other natural cloth, giving you the confidence to leave it on the table during the most boisterous family meals.

1 Take the raffia hanks apart and tie the ends together to make one large hank. **2** To make the leaf shapes, make three chains with the raffia, insert the crochet hook into the second chain and double crochet one stitch, turn the work around and double crochet into the first stitch, continue across in double crochet stitch to make three stitches in a row, and turn the work around and double crochet into the first stitch. Work across the row in double crochet to make four stitches, and continue turning the work and double crochet into the first stitch to increase the stitch in each row until there are ten stitches across. **3** Work one more row of ten stitches, turn the work and begin reducing one stitch from each row by skipping the first stitch in each row and working across in double crochet. The finished leaf shape will have twenty-one rows. **4** Work a slipstitch all the way along the edge, slip a knot into the last stitch at the tip of the leaf and cut off, leaving a tail of 8 in. Make twelve leaves in total. **5** Set a dry iron to a light heat setting and press each leaf on both sides to flatten. **6** Tidy up all the knots and raffia threads by pulling them through to the underside of each leaf and cutting off the stray ends. **7** Thread the needle with a thin, threadlike length of raffia and, working from tip to stem, stitch the beads in place, spacing them every other row apart in a straight line up the middle of each leaf. **8** Thread the needle with a new piece of threadlike raffia and bind one end of the sisal rope by wrapping the raffia tightly from the cut end ½ in. up the rope, then stitch through the rope and wind back down, stitch through the rope again, and knot in place. Repeat at the other end. **9** Mark the position of each leaf along the rope with a pencil. Sew each leaf in place using the tail of raffia left at the stem end. Keep all knots neat and to the back of the work. Sew the edges of the leaves where they touch with a basting stitch of raffia.

materials

Two 3 oz. hanks of natural raffia
120 small, green-glass pony beads
14½ in. length of ¼ in. sisal rope
Size H/8 crochet hook
Large-eyed sewing needle
Scissors
Pencil

round platter

This platter conjures up images of summertime and is perfect for serving up cold selections of savory foods and slices of sweet fresh fruit. Enjoy it for its simplicity of design—the stark definition of color and the contrasting elements of broken white tiles against rows of perfect red squares.

1 Sand the front and back surfaces of the plate to remove any varnish and "key" the surface for grouting. **2** Measure and mark the center of the plate and with the compass draw six consecutive circles, approximately 1 in. apart. This will give you seven rings, including the center dot. **3** Soak the red mosaic tiles in water for fifteen minutes and remove the backing paper. Leave to dry. Put the white tiles in a sack and smash with a hammer to get a variety of shapes and sizes. Using tile nippers, cut most of the red tiles into quarters. **4** Use the nippers to round off the edges of one whole red tile to go in the center of the plate. "Butter" the back of the tile with a little waterproof grout/adhesive applied with the artist's palette knife, and stick in place. **5** To make the next circle, apply grout to some of the white tile shards with the palette knife and press firmly in place. Work in sections around the ring, using the nippers to reshape tiles as needed to fit the design. **6** For the next circle, grout some red tile quarters and apply them, working around the circle. Continue working out to the edge of the plate, alternating the colors. Leave to set for twenty-four hours. **7** Spread grout over the entire surface with the grout spreader, filling in all gaps and crevices. Scrape the surface clear of all excess grout and wipe with a damp sponge until the tiled surface is clean. Wipe a smooth edge of grout around the outside edge, smoothing with a clean, damp sponge. Leave to set for twenty-four hours. **8** Turn the plate over and paint the bottom and any exposed edges with matte white emulsion paint. Leave to dry. **9** Wipe the tiled surface with a soft cloth and apply a thin coat of the floor wax. Leave to dry.

materials

Round wooden plate, 40¾ in.
in circumference, 12¾ in.
in diameter
Four 6 in. square white tiles
Four 4 in. square sheets of ¾ in.
square red glass mosaic tiles
Matte white emulsion paint
Waterproof grout/adhesive
Coarse sandpaper
Pair of compasses and pencil
Sack or strong trash bag
Hammer
Protective goggles
Tile nippers
Artist's palette knife
Grout spreader
Sponge
Paintbrush
Soft cloth
Clear floor wax

blanket mats

Blanket fabric provides excellent protection against hot plates for table surfaces. Blanket stitch is a traditional method of decorating and finishing the edges of applied shapes on such fabrics. By using bright colors and stylized shapes you can make a selection of cheerful place mats for an informal meal.

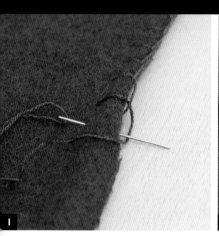 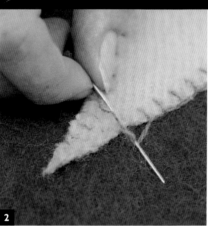 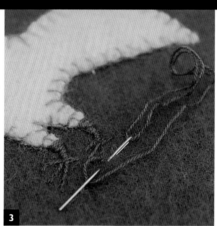 

materials

FOR EACH MAT
Blanket in main color
17¾ x 14 in.
Scraps of contrast color blanket
Fine wools in contrasting colors
Darning needle
Tracing paper
Pencil
Scissors
Sewing kit

1 Turn in the edges of the mat and blanket stitch to secure. **2** Make a template of the birds on page 243. Use this as a pattern to cut out the shapes from contrast blanket colors. Position each one on the mat and blanket stitch in place. **3** Use satin stitch and stem stitch to create the feet and a beak. **4** Make a large French knot in black for the pupil of the eye and stem stitch around this for the white of the eye.

frosted glass bowl

Floating candles illuminate this star-spangled bowl, making it a sophisticated centerpiece for a celebratory meal. When stenciling onto glassware, it is important to use glass paints, since normal emulsions and acrylics will not adhere and are therefore not suitable.

  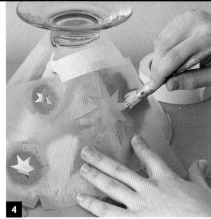 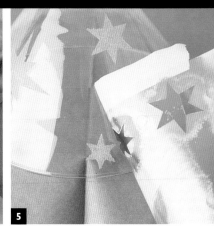

materials

Glass bowl of suitable design
Small pot of frosting varnish
Stencil film
Stencil brush
Craft knife and cutting mat
Masking tape
Lint-free cloth

1 Make two tracings of the star templates on page 245. Tape to the cutting mat, secure the stencil film over the top, and cut out with a craft knife. **2** Clean the glass thoroughly in warm, soapy water. **3** Dry the glass with a lint-free cloth. Make sure it is completely dry and free from dust before you begin stenciling. **4** Tape the larger star stencil into position using masking tape. Stipple with frosting varnish. Repeat, spacing the large star randomly around the bowl. Allow to dry. **5** Fill in any gaps as desired using the smaller star stencils.

aluminum mesh basket

Aluminum mesh is extremely soft, pliable, and easy to work with. Here it is pleated and tucked in place to form a basket and held in position with decorative wirework. Use it to serve amaretto cookies with after-dinner coffee, or fill it with chocolate eggs or sugared almonds at Easter.

materials

9 x 10 in. fine expanded aluminum mesh
5 x 3½ x 2½ in. bowl to use as a mold

Approximately 3 yd. of 16 gauge (0.05 in.) twisted galvanized wire
Approximately 3 yd. of 20 gauge (0.03 in.) twisted galvanized wire
Fine tinned copper wire
Scissors
Flat-ended modeling tool
Round-nose pliers
Wire cutters
Wooden spoon

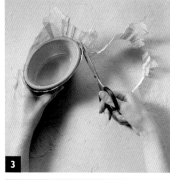

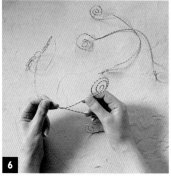
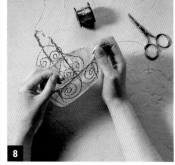
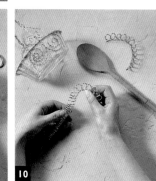
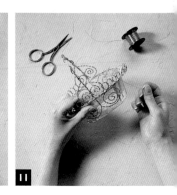

1 The galvanized wire should be twisted as you need it. (See page 11 for details on twisting.) **2** Lay out the piece of aluminum mesh. Center the bowl on the mesh. Mold the mesh to fit the outside of the bowl. Make six small tucks at each end to ensure a neat fit. Press firmly to hold the shape. **3** Carefully and evenly cut away the excess mesh from the rim of the bowl. Remove the bowl from the mesh form. **4** To strengthen the basket shape, cut a length of 16 gauge wire to fit exactly the top of the mesh form. Hold it in place and roll the top of the mesh over the wire. Push under with the modeling tool to secure. **5** For the handle, from 20 gauge wire, cut two lengths each 27½ in. and two lengths each 17¾ in. Using pliers, form a loose spiral at each end of each wire, with the spirals facing in the same direction. **6** Twist the straight section of the long lengths together to form the handle. Turn the spirals outward.

7 Bend back the neck of the spiral on the shorter lengths. Twist the shorter lengths one at a time onto the handle, turning the spirals inward. **8** Position the handle over the side of the basket. Bind on the spirals through the mesh using short lengths of tinned copper wire twisted tightly together. Secure the middle and each side of the spirals as well as the point at which the handle crosses the rim. Add sufficient joints to make the wire lie flat. **9** Secure the small spirals along the rim of the basket using tinned copper wire. Bind the spirals to the straight part of the handle, forming them into an upside-down heart. **10** Using the 20 gauge wire, make a coil by wrapping it around the handle of a wooden spoon. Flatten each loop and cut two lengths approximately 5 in. to fit along the basket rim at each side of the handle. **11** Bind the loop borders in place using tinned copper wire.

beaded fruit

Make a small group of a single fruit, such as pears, or make one of each type to fill a glass dish to create a wonderful alternative to the traditional fruit bowl centerpiece. Pressed cotton fruits are available from florist's suppliers. The sparkling fruits can be kept dust-free with a quick blow from a hair dryer.

 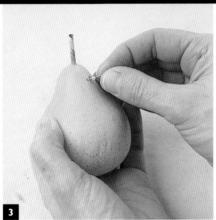  

materials

Pressed cotton fruit
Brass sequin and bead pins
Selection of seed beads
Crystal and gold-colored cup sequins
Thimble

1 Choose a selection of beads to match the color of the fruit and a selection of sequins. For the lemon, use clear and solid yellow beads, with a few cream and green beads to add depth. **2** On the pin, pick up a bead and then a sequin. **3** Press the pin into the fruit. It may be easier to use a thimble. **4** Each sequin should overlap the last slightly. As the fruits are already colored, small gaps between the sequins will not be noticeable. **5** Select beads and sequins in a random fashion using mainly crystal sequins to give the fruits a translucent appearance. Continue adding beads and sequins until the fruit is completely covered.

We spend more time on our homes at Christmas than at any other time of the year, filling it full of festive cheer with twinkling lights, colorful ornaments, and glittering stars. Good-quality decorations can be expensive, and it is perhaps more personal to make them yourself. The whole family can get involved with these projects that take a fresh look at traditional Christmas decorations. There is an original idea for tree lights, by creating angels out of

polypropylene, which lets the light shine through. There is also an inventive way to use up all those excess decorations that will not fit on the tree, and a design for making a herd of foil reindeer to grace any spare surface. None of the projects in this charming selection is particularly time-consuming, and each one will help you to create a thoroughly fresh and modern Christmas home.

christmas

folded-paper pinecones

These folded patchwork-style decorations are simple to make using a variety of pretty papers, polystyrene eggs, craft pins, and thread. A selection of beautifully textured handmade Thai and Indian papers were chosen, which are available in a wide range of colors and can be easily folded.

materials

A selection of 3 in. polystyrene eggs
Lightweight, handmade papers in a variety of colors (you need two for each egg)
Sequin and bead craft pins
Lamé embroidery thread
Straight edge or ruler
Paper scissors

1 On each of two sheets of contrasting color paper, measure and mark 1¾ in. wide strips down the length. Carefully cut each strip. **2** To make a folded triangle, on one strip, fold the corner of a short end in toward the long side so that the straight edges are aligned. Cut the excess strip away from the folded triangle. Make twenty-six from color A and twenty-four from color B. **3** Fold each triangle in half. **4** Cut one 1 in. square of color A. Cover the narrow end of the egg with the square and mold to fit. Pin the corners. **5** Place four triangles of color B over the paper square so that the triangle tips meet at the tip of the egg. Pin each triangle in place on the two narrow points using craft pins. Insert the pins at an angle. **6** Position four triangles of color A ¼ in. below the first row and pin in place so that the tips are staggered between the tops of the previous row. **7** Continue to alternate the colored rows, working around the form and keeping the triangles evenly spaced so that no gaps or pinheads show. **8** When you reach the end, carefully overlap the last four triangles. Cover all of the cut edges with a small square cut from the same color paper. Pin temporarily in place. **9** Make a lamé thread bow. Place on the end of the egg and pin through all the layers with a craft pin.

paper gift boxes

Beautifully packaged and presented gifts are always more appealing and add to the sense of occasion. Why not make these miniature boxes from beautiful handmade or textured papers, enclose a little gift inside, and slip them between the branches of the tree for an extra-special treat on Christmas.

materials

Heavyweight paper in your choice of colors
Ribbon or string
Double-sided tape
Paper punch
Scissors
Glue stick
Pen or pencil
Paper for templates

1 Enlarge the templates on pages 244–245 and cut out. To make large boxes, enlarge the templates in sections and stick the pieces together, overlapping and aligning lines as necessary. If you intend to make many boxes, use cardboard for the template. **2** Choose your paper for the box. On the wrong side, draw around the template. Mark all fold lines. Cut out the outline. **3** To make the pineapple box, crease all the fold lines. **4** Fold in the sides and secure the side tab on the inside of the box with double-sided tape. **5** Push in the bottom tab and secure as before. **6** Fill the box as desired. Interlink the pineapple top and bend the tab up into a standing position. **7** To make the cone box, crease all fold lines. Find the center of the long edge for the tip, then overlap the edges of the shape tightly to form a cone. Stick the side edge in position with double-sided adhesive tape. **8** Hold the cone with the point facing down. Fold each flap flat across the top. Secure the last flap with tape. Make a hole near the tip of the cone and thread ribbon or string through it.

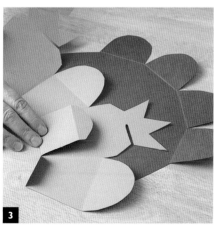

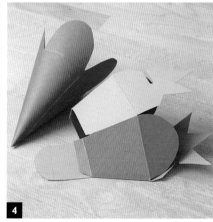

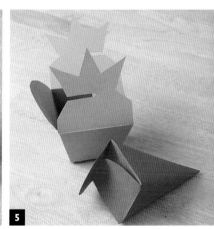

angel tree lights

Disguise your Christmas lights with this innovative design made from translucent polypropylene. Don't let the unusual material keep you from making these novel Christmas light cloches. They are easy to make and the materials are readily available from good craft suppliers.

materials

String of standard Christmas lights
Sheet of white polypropylene plastic
Template plastic or medium-weight cardboard
Scissors
Pencil
Tracing paper
Pinking shears
½ in. leather hole punch
Small piece of wood
Glue
Hammer
Paper punch

1 Photocopy the template on page 249. Glue the copy to cardboard and cut out. Punch the holes marked on the pattern using a paper punch. **2** Draw around the template on the white polypropylene plastic. Mark the holes and cutting lines. **3** Cut out each shape using pinking shears. Cut the head and arms with scissors. **4** With the piece of wood for the surface, use the leather punch and a hammer to punch the marked holes. **5** Wrap the wings around so that they overlap and slot together. **6** Align the holes in the wings and stick onto the Christmas lights so that they grip the rubber base of each light fitting.

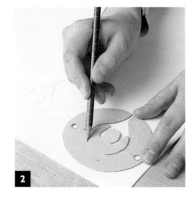

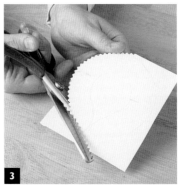

ribbon and ornament curtain

This novel curtain presents the perfect opportunity to use up all those ornaments that will not fit on the tree. It effectively adds a sparkle of Christmas color to an otherwise dull corner or cheers up an undecorated window. The effect is simple, uncluttered, and elegant.

 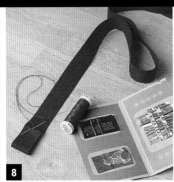   

materials

Variety of widths of grosgrain ribbon in assorted colors
Sewing thread to match ribbon colors
Assorted Christmas ornaments (one for each ribbon)
Paint to tone with ribbon colors
⅝ in. diameter dowel, to fit the width of the window, plus 1 in. on each side
Two screw eyes
Two screw hooks
Dressmaker's hooks and eyes (one for each ribbon)
Drill and saw
Masking tape
Paintbrush
Steel measuring tape
Sewing kit

1 Drill holes into the ends of the dowel and screw in screw eyes. **2** Measure and mark the dowel position on the window frame. Drill holes in alignment with the screw eyes and screw the hooks in place in the window frame. **3** Paint the ends of the dowel to match the main color of the ribbons. Allow to dry. **4** Arrange the ribbon lengths side by side on a flat surface. You will need enough to make up a curtain the same width as the width of the dowel. Number the ribbon lengths and make a chart detailing the order. **5** The middle ribbon hangs 12 in. above the window ledge. To gauge the length of this ribbon, measure the height of the window, then deduct 12 in. The shortest ribbons hang at each side of the window frame and are half the length of the middle ribbon. Mark the lengths on your chart. The remaining ribbons taper up from the middle to the sides. Work out suitable lengths for each and write them on your chart. **6** Add 2 in. to each length for seams. Drape the ribbons over the dowel and pin in place to check the fit. When you are happy with the arrangement, remove the dowel. **7** Stick small pieces of masking tape to the top of each ribbon, numbering them in order. Stitch any seams as necessary to prevent frayed edges. **8** Make a 2 in. loop in the top of one of the ribbons and, using a matching thread, sew it down. Make sure that the fold is straight; if it is crooked the ribbon will hang incorrectly. Sew all the ribbons in the same way. **9** To make the bottom edges, fold both corners to the back to form a point. Sew the turned in edges together, working from the point to the upper edge. **10** Sew a dressmaker's hook close to the tip of each ribbon at the back. **11** Slide all ribbons onto the dowel, keeping the correct numerical sequence. Hang at the window. **12** Hang a selection of Christmas ornaments onto the hooks at the back of the ribbons.

frosted window stencil

Frosted windows are an easy way to add a festive charm to your home. Your handiwork will be appreciated from both sides of the glazing. Making accurate stencils for the prancing deer, decorative foliage and flowers takes practice, but the effect is worth the effort.

1 Photocopy the three templates on pages 246–248, enlarging each to fit your window. You will need four flower and leaf designs and eight copies of the reindeer. **2** To make stencils, cut out each design on paper using the scalpel on a cutting mat. If you cut any lines in error, tape the piece together and continue cutting. **3** Clean the window panes thoroughly and allow to dry. **4** Place the stencils right side down on a sheet of newspaper. Spray lightly with spray mount and apply all the stencils to the window in the desired order. **5** Following the manufacturer's instructions, apply glass etch spray over the window surface. A soft, even coat applied twice works best. Allow to dry. **6** Peel away the stencils. **7** To remove the etch spray, scrape away with a single-edged razor or blade.

materials

Glass etch spray can
Large sheets of paper
Spray mount
Scalpel and cutting mat
Newspaper

christmas stockings

Kids will love these big felt Christmas stockings—especially when they're packed full of goodies. This project can be personalized with any number of decorative features, such as hand-embroidered snowflakes, punched holes, and felt leaves and berries applied using craft glue.

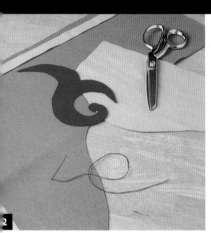

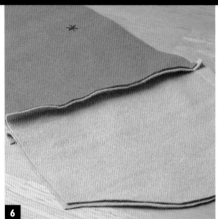

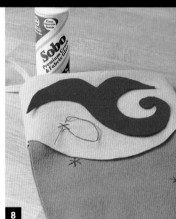

materials

20 in. x 1 yd. main color felt for the stocking

20 in. x 8 in. contrast color felt for the cuff

12 in. square contrast color felt for the cuff decoration

Hand and machine embroidery thread to match and contrast with the felt

Craft glue

Scissors

Sewing machine

Sewing kit

1 Enlarge the templates on page 250 on a photocopier to measure 17½ in. from the top to the bottom of the heel and cut out. Stick the patterns together, butting at the joint. **2** Draw around the stocking and the cuff on the correct color of felt. Cut two of each. **3** From scraps of cuff felt, cut a strip ½ x 8 in. Use this to make the hanging loop. **4** Embroider the six-point stars in a random pattern on the front and back of the stocking using three strands of contrasting embroidery thread. **5** With right sides together, stitch the top of each cuff to the top of each stocking. **6** Sew the cuff side seams together, pressing the selvage in the same direction on both sides. **7** Stitch the two halves of the stocking together using a ¼ in. seam. **8** Fold the cuff down. Embroider a six-point star on the cuff. Cut out the decoration in the contrast color and stick onto the cuff with craft glue. **9** Fold the hanging loop in half lengthwise. Sew through both layers from end to end using matching thread. Fold the loop in half and baste the two ends together. Sew in place inside the back of the cuff.

cut-paper shelf edging

We can probably all recall the fun of cutting paper snowflakes or crepe paper chains to make a Christmas display as children. This edging, though more sophisticated in appearance, is made using the same principle—lengths of paper folded over accordion-style, with shapes cut away from the folds.

materials

Roll of colored waxed paper
Roll of white or transparent waxed paper
Scalpel and cutting mat
Paper clips
Black marker
Pinking shears
Measuring tape
Glue

1 Measure the width of your shelf and determine the drop of the edging. Enlarge the template on page 249 to fit an even number of times into the shelf width. Define the cutout shapes with a black marker. For a long length, make several copies. 2 Cut the required length of colored and white waxed paper. Fold each length accordion-style to the same width as the template. 3 Slide the template between the third and fourth fold of the colored paper. Make sure that you can see the definition of the design lines through the top layer. Do not cut more that six layers at a time. 4 Secure all four corners of the stack with paper clips to keep the folds from slipping. 5 Place the stack on the cutting mat and carefully cut out the design. With a new, sharp blade you should be able to cut through six layers of paper and the template at the same time. Replace the blade regularly. Use a new template for each stack of six sheets. 6 Cut the scalloped edge with pinking shears. 7 Remove the paper clips and the paper template. 8 Slide a template inside the white waxed paper as before. Draw the scalloped edge with a pencil. Remove the template and cut on the line using pinking shears. 9 Unfold both accordions. Place the white cut paper behind the colored paper, all edges aligned. Now slide the white paper down so that it sits ½ in. below the colored paper. Stick the layers together. Fold the top edge over so that it creates a shelf lining, or cut it off and stick both layers of cut paper neatly to the edge of the shelf.

embossed velvet tablecloth

Sumptuous velvet in a rich jewel-like shade is perfect for the celebration of Christmas. All you need for this project is a hot iron and a rubber stamp. And while your instincts may tell you never to use a luxury fabric for a tablecloth, this one can be washed in the machine without fear of ruining the pile.

materials

1¼ yd. square of rayon or polyester velvet, or dimensions to suit your table
Sewing thread to match
Selection of 4–4½ in. rubber stamps
Iron
Workbench
Sewing kit

1 Select two or three large rubber stamp designs from a specialty stamp supplier. This tablecloth uses an arrangement of pomegranates, stylized acanthus leaves, and lush grapes to represent the bountiful display of the Christmas feast. **2** Decide on the approximate position of each stamp—make a sketch or mark the back of the velvet with a piece of chalk. Keep the pattern random. **3** Choose one stamp and clamp it to your workbench. This will keep the stamp from moving, which can cause double images. **4** Place the velvet over the rubber stamp, nap side down, where you want the image to appear. **5** Take a hot, dry iron and firmly press down onto the back of the velvet over the rubber stamp. Hold for five seconds. Use the heel of the iron, avoiding the steam holes as these will leave an impression. **6** Repeat this process with all the rubber stamps to complete your design. **7** To finish the edge of the tablecloth, roll in the edges of the velvet to the wrong side and blind hem stitch in place using matching thread.

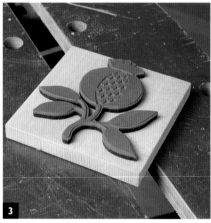
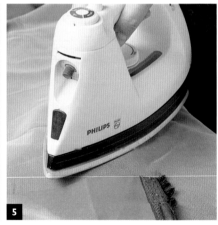

chocolate wreath

Chocolate ladybugs, bumblebees, and butterflies, and liqueur-encrusted orchard fruits create a modern reworking of the traditional wreath. The pine wreath is made from corrugated cardboard with the pine branches stuck in place using a glue gun. This is an enjoyable project to make that can be eaten, too!

 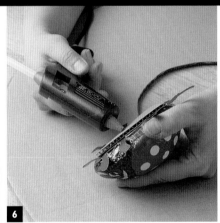  

materials

Two 22 in. squares of heavyweight corrugated cardboard, plus extra for the chocolates
Large bundle of pine branches
Foil-wrapped chocolates and wrapped candy—five or six very large and thirty medium or small, in assorted designs
Hot-glue gun and glue
Florist's wire
Plastic drinking straws
Scissors
Scalpel and cutting mat
Skewer or leather hole punch
Drawing pin and string
Pencil and ruler

1 Measure a 10 in. length of string. Tie one end to the pencil and the other to the drawing pin. Stick the pin in the center of one of the cardboard squares. Hold the pencil taut and draw a 20 in. diameter circle. Center a second circle inside the first, 8 in. in diameter. Cut out and discard the center and outer edges. **2** Place the wreath on the second piece of cardboard with the corrugated lines in opposite directions. Stick the cut shape to the uncut board using a hot-glue gun. Allow to dry. Cut out the second piece of cardboard. **3** Using the point of a skewer, make two holes 3 in. from the edge of the cardboard wreath and 3 in. apart. **4** Push one straw through each hole until the end is flush with the surface at the back of the board. Cut off the excess. Glue in place and allow to dry. The straws keep the hanging wires from tearing the cardboard. **5** Cut one 10 in. length of wire and thread through both holes. Twist the ends together at the back of the wreath to form a hanging wire. **6** Glue the largest chocolates to scraps of cardboard and stick in an even pattern on the front of the wreath. **7** Cut long twigs of pine to cover the inside edge of the wreath. Cut shorter twigs to fit between the chocolates. Stick each in place using the hot-glue gun. Add twigs to the outside, radiating out from the center. Keep the edges neat and even. Cover any bare areas. **8** Glue the remainder of the chocolates and candy onto the pine twigs.

twisted wire decorations

These simple candy-striped Christmas tree decorations incorporate wirework skills on a small scale. Create the candy stripe by twisting a strand of pink anodized aluminum wire into the structure of the scrolls and complement the color scheme with attractive glass beads.

 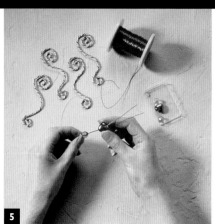  

materials

**Roll of 16 gauge (0.05 in.)
galvanized wire
Small reel of 24 gauge (0.02 in.)
pink anodized aluminum wire
Glass beads: two small iridescent,
one red heart, two pink cut-glass
Wire cutters
Bent-nose pliers
Small scissors
Hand drill
Wooden spoon**

1 Cut two long lengths from both wires. Twist the aluminum wire by bending it in half around a fixed point such as a baluster and feed the two cut ends into the chuck of a hand drill. Tighten to secure the ends. Keep the wire taut and turn the drill in a clockwise direction, twisting the wire to the required tension. Undo the chuck to release the wire. **2** Bend the galvanized wire in half around the fixed point and tighten all the ends of both wires around a wooden spoon handle by twisting them in a counterclockwise direction. Pull the wire taut, and keeping it horizontal, twist the wire by turning the spoon handle clockwise. When it is twisted as tightly as you require, carefully release the spoon and cut the wire free with wire cutters. **3** Cut four lengths of twisted wire each 8½ in. with the wire cutters. **4** Form one end of each length into a large, loose spiral. Make a curve in the central section, then form a tight spiral at the other end. Make four. **5** Cut one length of pink wire 8½ in. Thread a small iridescent bead halfway along. Bend the wire in two around the bead, then thread the remaining beads onto both wires, following the order in the main photograph. **6** Put the four scrolls together, with the bend facing outward. Place the beaded wire in the center of the large scroll. Tightly bind the top joint approximately eight times with pink wire. **7** Twist the ends together to secure. Bind the base in the same manner. **8** Open out the shape, making sure that the scrolls are evenly spaced.

The raised pattern that catches and reflects the shimmering light is made by drawing on the back of the soft aluminum foil with a ballpoint pen.

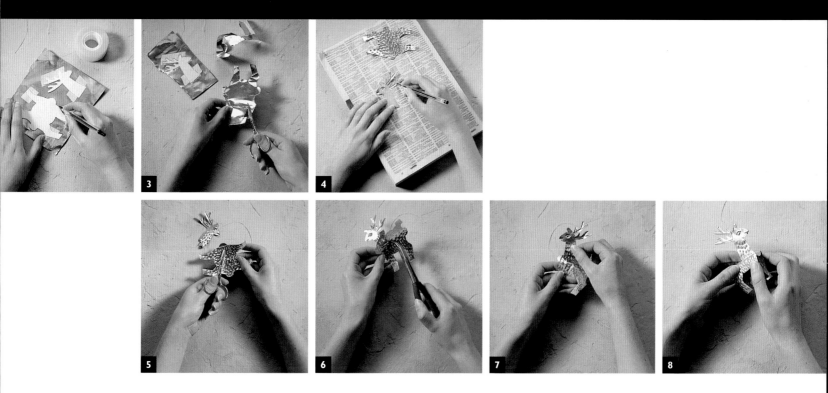

1 Photocopy the templates on page 250. Stick the copy on cardboard and cut out. 2 Tape the templates onto the aluminum foil. Draw around each outline. 3 Remove the templates. Carefully cut out each shape using small-pointed scissors. Take special care with the antlers. 4 Place the shapes on the telephone book. Mark the body pattern by pressing with a dry ballpoint pen. Mark short lines along the back and then at right angles down the legs. Mark the eye, mouth, antlers, and neck. Cut a ¼ in. slit at each side of the base of the neck, ¼ in. up from the base. Turn the cut sections in and press flat. 5 Make a slit in the front of the reindeer body large enough to fit the the base of the neck through. Push the neck through the slit. 6 To secure the head firmly to the body, turn the body to the wrong side and use the pliers to open out the folded-in sections. 7 Bend the tab at the front of the body down. 8 Bend the body over to enable the reindeer to stand.

materials

Aluminum foil, 6 in. square for each reindeer
Tracing paper and pencil
Thin cardboard and glue
Dry ballpoint pen
Transparent tape
Small-pointed scissors
Old telephone book
Bent-nose pliers
Transparent tape

mistletoe kissing bough

Sprigs of mistletoe are entwined with delicate curling, twisted wires and gentle ringing bells. The two wire circles are held together with simply constructed springs and the whole structure is suspended from the ceiling with a huge wire bow—the perfect shelter for a Christmas kiss.

materials

1 lb. of 12 gauge (0.08 in.)
galvanized steel wire
1 lb. of 18 gauge (0.04 in.)
galvanized steel wire
Very fine florist's or beading wire
Twenty-four small silver bells
Round-nose pliers
Flat-nose pliers
Wire cutters
Pencil
Large bunch of mistletoe

1 For the two wire circles, cut two lengths from the 12 gauge wire, one 44 in. and one 68 in. **2** Using round-nose pliers, and beginning at one end, form four loops in the longer length of wire, each 15 in. apart. Twist the opposite end around and thread through the first loop to form a circle. **3** Repeat with the second length of wire, this time making the loops 11½ in. apart. **4** From 18 gauge wire, cut eight lengths 1¾ yd. long and twelve lengths 36 in. **5** Make eight springs with the 1¾ yd. lengths of wire. To form a spring, wrap the length of wire tightly around a pencil. Slide the coil from the pencil and open out the last loop at each end. Stretch the coils to form four short springs and four longer springs. **6** Attach the shorter springs to the loops in the small wire wreath. Attach the opposite ends to the loops in the larger wire wreath. **7** Attach the four long springs to the loops in the small wreath to hang over the top. Twist the opposite ends together with a scrap of wire. **8** Using two 36 in. lengths of wire, form a bow, leaving 12 in. tails. Twist in a loop at the knot point. Wrap the tails tightly around a pencil to form springs and pull into the desired position. Attach one silver bell to the end of each. Make four bows. **9** Using the remaining four lengths of wire, make one large bow for the top for the wreath. Add bells as before. **10** Cut a 4 in. length of 18 gauge wire. Thread the wire through the large bow and the four springs. Twist the ends together. **11** To make

the hanging wire, from 18 gauge wire, cut one length 24 in. Form a spring with half of it, then bend the other half into a hook. Attach the spring to the top of the large bow and use the hook to hang the bough. **12** To make four jump rings, from 18 gauge wire, cut one length 4 in. Wrap tightly around a pencil. Remove the pencil. Using wire cutters, snip the spring, cutting complete single circles of wire.

Use these to attach the four small bows to the bottom loops in the larger wreath. Bend the two ends shut. **13** Cut twigs of mistletoe into 15 in. forked lengths. Use fine wire to attach the mistletoe in layers to the two wreaths as shown in the photograph above. Wrap securely, as mistletoe shrinks as it dries.

To make the most of lazy summer days, we need suitable garden furniture and accessories—the hammock to string up between two trees, the picnic cloth to spread under a leafy bough with a couple of generously sized floor cushions, and the parasol changing tent that can be put to a wide variety of uses, from a children's den to a quiet spot for lazy afternoons. Outdoor living is about entertaining, too, and this chapter provides ideas for a tablecloth

weighted with beaded tassels to keep it from being blown away by a gust of wind, covers for directors' chairs that can be brought up around the table for informal seating, and garden candles to extend our enjoyment well into the evening. And for those who want to be active, there are ideas for window boxes and hanging baskets.

outdoor living

parasol changing tent

This innovative project uses a sturdy white canvas parasol—now a familiar sight on patios, balconies, and gardens—as the structure, with eight panels of fabric attached to the rim. It can adopt a range of roles from a changing tent to a hideaway for quiet reading or an instant shady spot.

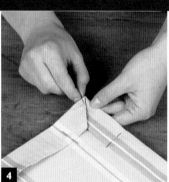
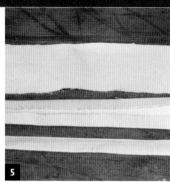

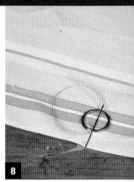

materials

Octagonal garden parasol
12 yd. fabric to match
Sewing thread to match
Forty-eight curtain rings
Sewing machine
Sewing kit

1 Cut eight panels 33½ x 86¼ in. To adapt the panels to fit your parasol, measure the width of each parasol section and the height from the rim to the ground. **2** Press a ¼ in. seam all around each panel. Turn in another 1¼ in. and press. **3** Miter the corners: Unfold the seams and turn in the corners. Clip the diagonal, leaving a small seam allowance. Turn in the seam. Refold the edges. **4** Press, then hand stitch the miter. Machine stitch the seams. **5** To make the ties, cut forty strips 2 x 22½ in. Turn in ½ in. at each short end. Press. Fold each strip in half lengthwise. Press. Open out the fold. Turn in the raw edges to the center fold. Refold, then stitch across each short end and down the long edge. **6** Fold one tie in half and pin to the top right-hand corner of the wrong side of one panel. Add a second tie to the top center. Stitch in place. To the top left-hand side stitch a curtain ring. **7** Stitch three ties at even intervals to the left-hand side of the panel. **8** Stitch three curtain rings to correspond on the right-hand side. Repeat for the other seven panels. **9** Sew corresponding rings around the rim of the parasol and tie the panels in place.

hammock

A hammock strung between two trees is the epitome of relaxation in the outdoors. It is easy to make.
You need just a couple of lengths of wood, with a dozen holes drilled into each at regular intervals,
and some sturdy rope threaded through eyelets into each end of a length of strong fabric.

materials

3 yd. of 54 in. wide yellow and
green canvas
20 yd. of ½ in. wide rope
Two wooden battens 1 yd. long
with twelve evenly spaced
holes drilled in large enough to
thread the rope through
Two steel rings 2–3 in.
in diameter
Twenty-six eyelets and
eyelet kit
Sewing machine
Sewing kit

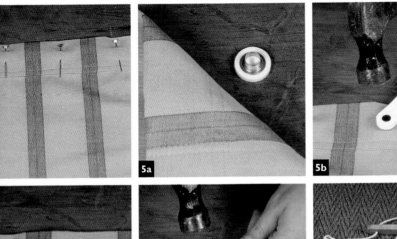

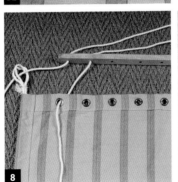

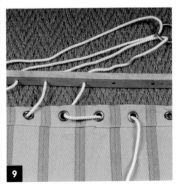

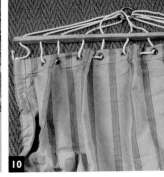

1 Square up the fabric. Turn in ¾ in. across the width for the top and bottom. Press. Turn in another 2 in. and press. Double topstitch in place. **2** Repeat step 1 to hem the sides. **3** Find the center of the top and bottom seams and mark with a pin. This is the position of the center eyelet. **4** Measure and mark with pins the position of six evenly spaced eyelets to each side of the center pin. **5** Insert the eyelets following the manufacturer's instructions. (see step pictures 5a–d) **6** Thread a double thickness of rope through each side seam. Make a knotted loop at each end. **7** With a third length of rope, leaving a long thread end, begin at the left-hand side and thread the rope through the loop then through the first hole of the batten working from bottom to top. **8** Thread the rope through the metal ring above the center of the batten, back down through the second hole in the batten, then up through the first eyelet. **9** Thread the rope through the next two eyelets and up through the wooden batten to the ring. Repeat. **10** Bring the rope back down through the batten and through the next eyelet. Catch in the next two eyelets before threading back up to the ring. Repeat across the hammock. **11** Finish at the right-hand side by threading the rope through the batten and ring and knot the end of the rope around the loop at the end of the side seam. **12** Repeat at the other end of the hammock to finish.

floor cushion

By its nature, a floor cushion should be designed for a fair amount of wear and tear without forsaking appearance. Here, sky-blue linen is secured with contrasting colored fabrics machine stitched in place and then decorated with chunky woollen blanket stitch.

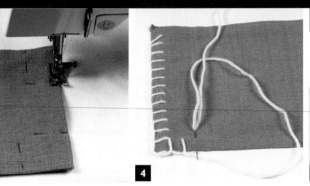

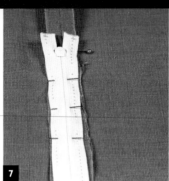

materials

**Large cushion pad,
26¼ x 26¼ in.
1¾ yd. blue linen
18 x 18 in. white
cotton union
Matching sewing thread
One skein each of blue and
white wool
22 in. white zipper
Sewing machine
Sewing kit**

1 Cut two blue squares 28 in. for the cushion front and back. **2** For the appliqué decoration, cut one white square 17½ x 17½ in., and one blue square 7½ x 7½ in. **3** Press under ¾ in. around the raw edge of each appliqué square. Trim the diagonal at each corner to reduce the bulk. Center the small blue square on the white square. Pin and machine stitch close to the edge. **4** Decorate the edge with blanket stitch. **5** Repeat to stitch the white square to the cushion front. **6** To insert the zipper, pin and baste the cushion front and back right sides together along one edge. Measure and mark the centered zipper position. Machine stitch the cushion front and back together at each side of the zipper position, taking a ¾ in. seam. **7** Press the seam open. On the seam, position the zipper right side down over the basted area. Pin. Using a zipper foot, stitch the zipper in position without catching the teeth of the zipper. **8** Open the zipper slightly. Stitch the cushion front to the cushion back using a ¾ in. seam and rounding the corners. Overcast the raw edges. Turn right side out. Press and insert the cushion pad.

patchwork picnic cloth

Patchwork at its simplest, this is a fast and easy project for you to make. The shapes are big and easy to handle, requiring only straight line seams, and the embellishment is running stitch. The beauty of this cloth is the colors of effervescent pink and orange surrounded with a bright lime-green border.

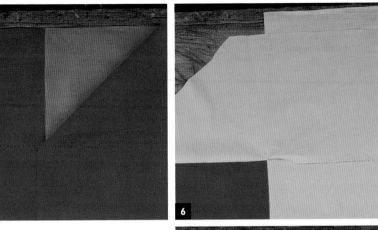

materials

2 yd. lime-green cotton fabric
1 yd. orange cotton fabric
1 yd. pink cotton fabric
Sewing thread to match
1¾ yd. of 54 in. wide
calico for backing
Thick navy thread
Ruler
Pencil
Sewing machine
Sewing kit

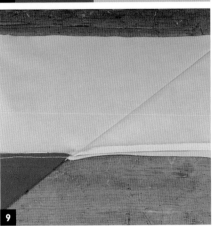

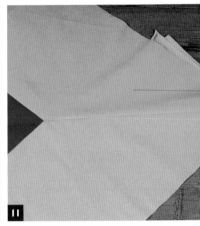

1 Cut six pink and six orange rectangles, 9½ x 15¾ in. **2** For the border, cut two lime-green strips 166 x 10¾ in. and two 156½ x 10¾ in. **3** On a clean, flat surface, arrange the pink and orange rectangles, four wide and three deep, alternating the colors throughout. **4** Using a ¼ in. seam allowance, stitch the rectangles into the three rows. **5** Stitch the three rows together. **6** Along one long edge of each border, find and mark the center point with a pin. Find the center of each side of the cloth and match the two points. With right sides together, pin each border to the cloth, allowing the excess to overlap at each corner. **7** Stitch each border in place. Begin stitching ¼ in. from the raw edge of the cloth. **8** To miter the corners, press under the ¼ in. seam allowance on the inside raw edge of each border. **9** Fold the cloth diagonally at each corner and, with a pencil and ruler, draw a diagonal line at an accurate forty-five-degree angle. Baste along the line, then open out the cloth and make sure the miter lies flat. Adjust as necessary. **10** Machine stitch the miter. Trim away the excess border. **11** The border is 8 in. wide. Turn in the excess and press. Fold in a diagonal at each corner across the point where the two pressed lines cross. Trim away the corners, leaving a small seam. Refold the seams and stitch the miter. **12** With navy thread, sew the running stitch decoration. **13** Cut the backing ½ in. smaller than the cloth. Turn in a seam and press. Slipstitch the backing in place.

lavender flower box

An ordinary window box is disguised with woven lavender cuttings, then planted up to create a truly heady display. Try other aromatic cuttings such as sage, thyme, rosemary, and marjoram. If you do not have enough of one variety, use different stems in combination.

 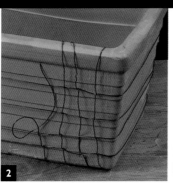   

materials

Plastic or terra-cotta window box
Large quantity of fresh lavender
Garden wire
Pliers
Florist's scissors
Heavy-duty polythene for the flower box liner

1 Wind lengths of garden wire in parallel horizontal bands around the base of the window box. Secure each length by twisting the ends around each other. Do not make the bands too tight or you will find it impossible to thread the lavender. **2** Repeat to make vertical bands by centering each length under the base of the window box and weaving the remaining sections through the horizontal bands to make a grid and hooking the ends over the top. **3** Using the longest stalks, thread the lavender vertically through the grid all around the box. **4** Repeat, weaving the stalks horizontally until you have a close weave. **5** Trim the vertical stalks flush with the top edge of the box. **6** Use the trimmed stalks to fill any gaps. **7** Gently ease the woven lavender away from the base. **8** Line the box with heavy-duty plastic and make some drainage holes in the base. Put the lavender box in position in your garden before filling with potting compost and planting up.

plant name marker

For those of us who plant a flower only to be unable to identify it months later because we have lost the name tag, these plant markers are the perfect solution. Copper, with its warm color, complements the infinite palette of greens found among foliage in the house or garden.

materials

Fine copper foil
Tracing paper
Pencil
Thin cardboard
Glue
Ballpoint pen
Two different-sized tracing wheels
Star punch
Hammer
Small-pointed scissors
Transparent tape
Old telephone book
Small block of wood

1 Trace or photocopy the template on page 250. Stick the copy to cardboard and cut out. Tape the tracing to copper foil and draw around it with the pen to make an indent. Cut out the shape. **2** Place on an old phone book. Draw around the edge with the small tracing wheel, pressing firmly to create the indented dotted line. The pattern will appear as a raised design on the right side of the key.

3 In the same way, roll the larger tracing wheel along the middle of the "stem" to produce a similar pattern. **4** Place the plant marker on a piece of wood. Position the star punch at the top, then at the base of the central section. Hit with the hammer to transfer the design. **5** To finish, using the directory for a surface, write the name of the plant on the right side in the central section with a ballpoint pen.

garden candles

Candle making has become such a popular activity that you should be able to find most of the necessary materials at your local art and craft stores. Display your outdoor candles in an assortment of glassware found in the kitchen, such as drinking glasses, glass jars, and old vases.

1 Collect all your materials together. Protect your work surfaces with newspaper. **2** Heat up your glass containers by standing them in a tray of warm water, then place in the oven at the lowest temperature setting. Leave until ready to fill with the melted wax. Ensure that the insides of the containers do not get wet. **3** Melt the candle wax and beeswax slowly in a double boiler or place one saucepan inside another. **4** For one container, cut a length of wick the depth of your container plus approximately 2 in. extra for tying on the sustainer and slug and winding around the pencil. **5** Attach a sustainer to one end of the wick and fix in place by crimping the neck with the pliers. **6** Thread on the slug so that it sits on top of the sustainer. The weight will help keep the wick in the correct position. **7** When the wax has melted, allow it to cool to approximately 158°F. Add any fragrances or insect repellents as needed at this point and stir in gently. **8** Holding the wick so that it hangs just above the bottom of the container, pour the melted wax into the warm container. **9** Wind the end of the wick around a thin rod or pencil so that it is taut and rest the pencil on top of the container. **10** As the wax cools, it shrinks in the middle, making a well. To keep this from happening, use the knitting needle to prick the center every ten minutes until set. After approximately an hour, top up with melted wax. **11** When the wax is hard, trim the wick.

materials

Candle-making wax

Beeswax

Nylon wicks

Sustainers and slugs (weights)

Fragrances/insect repellents

Pencil (or thin rod)

Thin knitting needle or similar

Glass containers

Double boiler or old saucepans

Long-nose pliers

Cooking thermometer

Scissors

Newspaper

window box

Use a simple mosaic design to give a window box or flowerpot a boost. Using frostproof grout and adhesive will protect the mosaic surface of the window box against the elements, allowing you to leave it outside all year round. The pleasing design will always look good, even if it is only filled with greenery.

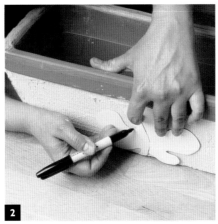
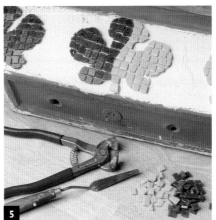

1 Mix frostproof adhesive with water to a spreadable consistency. With a palette knife and grout spreader, cover the outside of the window box with a thin, even coat of frostproof adhesive. This will keep any lime from seeping out through the clay and give you a flat, even surface to work on. Leave to set for twelve hours. **2** Photocopy the leaf templates on page 252, adjusting the size to fit the height dimension of your window box if necessary. Glue the photocopies to thin cardboard and cut out. Hold the templates in position on the sides of the window box and draw around them with a permanent marker. **3** Remove all the tiles from their backing paper by soaking them in water first; after fifteen minutes the paper will slip off easily. Spread the tiles on newspaper to dry. **4** Cut half of the two green colored tiles into quarters with tile nippers. The rest you may need for cutting odd shapes: Cut as you need them. **5** Begin to mosaic the central leaf design from the inside line to one outside edge in one shade of green and then the other half in the other shade of green. Trim and shape the tiles as you need to. "Butter" the backs with a small amount of the tile adhesive on the end of an artist's palette knife and stick them firmly in position. **6** Complete all the leaf shapes and leave to dry for twenty-four hours. **7** For the background, cut most of the pale pink tiles into quarters with the tile nippers. Stick on the tile pieces as before around the leaf patterns, creating even, horizontal rows as you go. Nip and cut the pieces as needed. Work all the way around the window box leaving the top rim free of pattern. Leave to set for twelve to twenty-four hours. **8** Cut the rest of the pale pink tiles into quarters and each of the dark pink tiles into three strips. Apply in a horizontal striped pattern around the entire rim of the window box, nipping and trimming tiles as needed. Leave to set for twenty-four hours. **9** Mix the frostproof grout to a thick, creamy consistency and apply to the entire tiled surface of the box, scraping it across the surface to fill all cracks and gaps and blending around the edges. Scrape off the excess grout and wipe the surface with a clean, damp sponge. Keep wiping until the tiles come clean. **10** Smooth some grout over the top rim of the window box to avoid the contrast of the terra-cotta clay. Smooth this edge over with a clean, damp sponge. Leave to dry for twenty-four hours. **11** Wipe the tiled surface of the window box with a soft cloth and then apply a thin coat of clear floor wax. Leave to dry.

materials

Clay window box 16 x 16½ in.
Four 4 in. square tiles in each color
of lime and grass green
Ten 4 in. square pale, dusky pink,
clay tiles
Two 4 in. square, dark dusky pink
tiles
Frostproof adhesive
Frostproof grout
Grout spreader
White school glue
Thin cardboard
Scissors
Permanent marker
Artist's palette knife
Newspaper
Protective goggles
Tile nippers
Sponge
Soft cloth
Clear floor wax

beaded table runners

The design of this simple pair of runners makes a feature of the seams, bringing the turning to the right side. The raw linen is then subtly embellished with lines of small hand-carved wooden beads strung along the short sides that hang down on either side of the table.

1 Turn in ¼ in. all around the linen edge. Press. Turn in another 1 in. Press. Unfold the turnings. **2** Turn in each corner. Clip the fabric at a diagonal to reduce the bulk, leaving a small seam allowance. **3** On a remnant of fabric, fray the threads and pull away several lengths on which to thread the beads. **4** Knot one bead onto the end of a 16 in. length of thread. **5** String several beads and make a knot in the thread to hold them in place. To leave a gap, make a large knot and continue threading beads. **6** Stitch the lengths of beaded thread at equal intervals to the second fold line and make a knot so that the thread end will be caught in the seam. **7** Refold the table runner seams and hand stitch the miter. **8** Machine stitch the seam in place ¾ in. from the folded edge.

materials

TO MAKE ONE RUNNER
22¾ x 63 in. natural colored linen
plus extra for thread
Matching thread
A selection of carved wooden beads
Sewing machine
Sewing kit

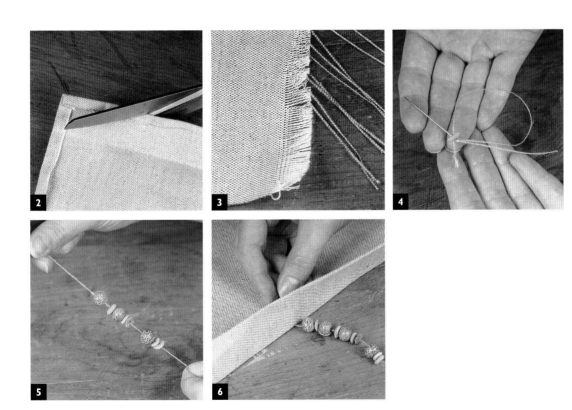

buttoned place mats

These stripe-on-stripe place mats are constructed from two rectangles of fabric secured with four dainty shell buttons at each corner. So easy, a full set can be machine stitched in an afternoon. The design is pleasant and can be comfortably used for an informal lunch or as settings for an evening meal.

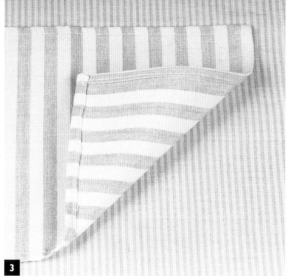

materials

FOR ONE PLACE MAT
18 x 14¼ in. narrow blue striped
fabric
12 x 9 in. wide blue striped fabric
Four shell buttons
Sewing machine
Sewing kit

1 Turn in and press ¼ in. along each raw edge of the narrow blue striped fabric. Turn in another ¼ in. and press. Machine stitch to hold. **2** Repeat with the wide blue striped decorative rectangle. **3** Center the decorative rectangle on the place mat and pin in place. **4** Position a button at each corner and hand stitch in place through all the layers. Remove the pins and press the finished place mat.

director's chair loose cover

The canvas back and seating of director's chairs can become grubby over time. Give them a new lease on life with a fabric that coordinates with other pieces of garden furniture. For easy maintenance, use only quality cotton fabrics that can be washed at high temperatures.

materials

Pink, orange, and purple
Madras check
Sewing thread to match
Sixteen eyelets, 1 in.
in diameter
Large sheets of paper
Sewing machine
Sewing kit

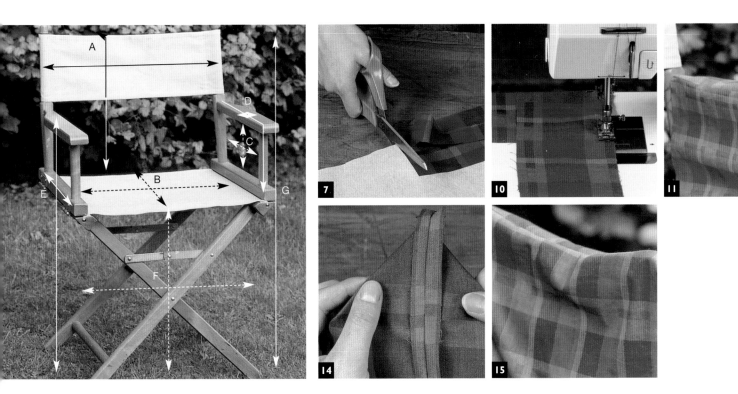

1 Measure the height and width of the front of the chair back. Add on the thickness of the chair sides and top (A). **2** Measure the depth and width of the seat (B). Add 14½ in. to the depth. **3** Measure the width and drop from the top of the arm to the seat (C); the width of the arm and the length from the back to the chair (D); and the width and drop from the top of the arm to the floor (E). Add 15 in. to the width of E. Double the fabric quantity for C, D, and E—one set for each side. **4** Measure the width of the chair and the drop from the front of the seat to the floor (F), then measure the back of the chair from the top to the floor (G). Add 15 in. to the width of F and G. **5** To all your measurements add a generous ½ in. seam all around, except for hem edges of E, F, and G. Add 4 in. hem. **6** With the patterns, make a mock-up to ensure a good fit without straining the seams. **7** Cut each pattern from the fabric. **8** Cut eight ties 14 x 3¼ in. from the fabric. **9** Center the base of A to the back of B. Make a pleat 2½ in. deep in B, parallel to A. Sew the pleat, then keep the pleat free during assembly. **10** Sew D to the top and front edge of C. Stitch to within a seam allowance width of the corner of C. Lift the presser foot. Rotate, then realign D and stitch the second side in place. **11** Try the fit over the arm. Make

another in reverse. **12** Stitch the lower edge of C to B. Sew the vertical of C to the cutout edge of A. Sew the end of D to the top of the cutout (it does not complete the cutout). Repeat at both sides. **13** Press in a double 1¼ in. in seam at both sides of E, F, and G. Unfold the hems and keep clear of the stitching. Sew the top of E across the cutout on A, along D, and down the front edge of D. Repeat on the other arm. Center F to B and sew, continuing across the lower ends of D. **14** Center the top of G to A and sew. With the hem edges of E and G level, sew G to E and A at the sides from a point level with seam B–F on the front upward. **15** To make the fabric fit at the top of the chair, form a triangle shape on each side seam to align with the top seam. Stitch across the triangle at right angles 1 in. from the point. Test the fit. **16** Sew the pressed hems on the sides of the openings. Press a 2 in. double hem on all lower edges. **17** Add eyelets through the hems following the instructions for the hammock (see page 203). **18** To make the ties, press in a seam at the short ends. Press in ½ in. along each long edge. Fold in half lengthwise and press again. Stitch around the ties. Once the cover is on the chair, thread the ties through the eyelets and tie.

hanging flower basket

By making this wire basket with lots of points and dangling clusters of silver beads, it becomes an object of beauty that looks just as attractive when left empty as when it is brimming with a careless array of glorious summer flowers.

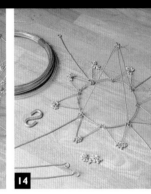

materials

Thirty-two bell cluster beads
Six bumblebee beads
Roll of fine beading wire,
24 gauge (0.02 in.)
16 oz. galvanized wire,
12 gauge (0.08 in.)
16 oz. galvanized wire,
14 gauge (0.06 in.)
3 in. S hook
Round-nose pliers
Needle-nose pliers
Wire cutters

1 Cut all the wire lengths for the basket with wire cutters as follows. Bottom circle: one length of 12 gauge wire 29½ in. long. Top circle: one of length of 12 gauge wire 37 in. long. Bottom struts: six lengths of 12 gauge wire 8¼ in. long. Decorative edging: thirty-two lengths of 14 gauge wire 15 in. long. Sides of basket: twenty-four lengths of 12 gauge wire 8 in. long. Hanging chain: eight lengths of 12 gauge wire 9 in. long. Crown circle: one length of 12 gauge wire 20 in. long. **2** To make the top and bottom circles, take each length of wire in turn and close the circle shape by twisting 5 in. at each end around each other with the needle-nose pliers. The top ring should measure 9½ in. in diameter and the bottom ring 17 in. **3** Take the wire for the bottom struts, straighten them out, and using the round-nose pliers, bend the ends into open loops, curving in the same direction. Attach the wires in an even crisscross pattern to the bottom circle, like the spokes of a wheel, tightly closing all connecting loops. **4** To secure, take a length of fine beading wire and wrap it around the circumference of the circle, enclosing the end of the struts as you wrap. **5** Take the length for the decorative edging, and with the round-nose pliers, bend each in the middle to form a V. Put a cluster of bell beads on each and bend the ends into open loops, curving toward the back of the shape to make it three-dimensional, rather than flat at the sides. **6** Attach twelve beads to the bottom circle by securing the loops shut with the needle-nose pliers, placing one V-shape in the gaps between the struts. **7** Take the wire for the sides of the basket. Leave them in an arched shape and make open-ended loops at both ends, curving them toward the outside of the arc shape, with the round-nose pliers. **8** Attach to the bottom circle into every space between a V-shape and a strut. Ensure that the arcs curve inward.

Close all bottom loops with the needle-nose pliers. **9** Attach all the top loops to the top circle by crisscrossing every pair of side arcs and then closing the loops with the needle-nose pliers. **10** Attach twelve *V* shapes to the top circle inside the crisscrosses of the side arcs. Keep the spacing between the side arcs even. Close all loops securely with the needle-nose pliers. **11** Cut six lengths of 14 in. beading wire, string on a bumblebee bead, and wrap the wire around alternate cross sections of the side arcs. Tighten securely and tie off on the inside of the basket. **12** To make the crown, twist the ends of the wire over each other to form a circle 15 in. in diameter. Attach eight *V*-shaped pieces of decorative edging. Space them evenly and close all loops with needle-nose pliers. **13** Flatten out the lengths of wire for the hanging chain and bend loops into each end using round nose pliers. Turn all the loops in the same direction. **14** Attach four lengths of "chain" wires to the crown, securing one end of each between every two *V* shapes. Attach the remaining four lengths of chain directly into the loops of the four previous ones. Close the loops firmly. **15** Check that the chain wires are hanging properly, four hanging down and four going up. Attach the four hanging down to the top edge of the basket, spacing them evenly between every four *V*-shapes and closing all loops. **16** Gather the four top hanging chains onto the S hook and hang the basket in place.

bead-embroidered cushion

To add a little sparkle to entertaining outdoors, make up cushions in natural fabrics, such as a raw silk dressmaker's cloth, blending in shades of embroidery thread and beads. Choose a fabric with a slightly rough weave to accentuate the contrast of fine, simple embroidery stitches and glittering beads.

materials

12 in. square of machine-washable cushion
18 in. x 45 in. raw silk
Four 8 yd. hanks of embroidery thread
2 oz. size 6/0 colored seed beads
Pencil
Embroidery needles
Tracing paper
Tracing wheel
Dressmaker's tracing carbon paper
Sewing machine
Sewing kit

1 Add a border of 3½ in. to the size of your cushion and cut two pieces of silk to this measurement (19 in.). **2** Photocopy the border pattern on page 251 to the correct size and trace it onto tracing paper. **3** Place on top of the dressmaker's carbon paper and pin in place to one side of one piece of fabric, leaving a seam allowance of ½ in. Transfer the pattern to the fabric using a tracing wheel. Mark the pattern around all four sides of fabric. **4** Lay the fabric on a flat surface. Split a workable length of embroidery thread into three strands. Thread an embroidery needle (the correct size to get the beads over), double the thread over, and knot the end. **5** Embroider the pattern in an even running stitch, threading on beads where indicated in the pattern. **6** Take both pieces of fabric and place right sides together. Sew a seam ½ in. from the edge around three sides. Turn the cover right side out and press in the fourth hem. Iron all edges. **7** Measure and mark with pins 3 in. in from the edge of the three sewn sides to hold both sides of the fabric in place. Sew around this inner border. Slip the cushion in and sew up the fourth side, along the inside and outside edges of the border. **8** Finally, thread the needle with all six strands of embroidery thread and make two lines of running stitch ¼ in. apart, over the top of the stitching on the inside of the border and around the outer edge, as shown.

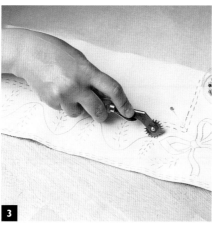

tasseled tablecloth

The colors and stripes in the fabric of this cloth bring to mind exotic, spicy foods, barbecues, and brightly colored cocktails. The vivid arrangements of plastic beads catch the light and also serve to weigh the cloth down and keep any windy weather in check.

materials

57½ in. square piece of print or
stripe cotton cloth
57½ in. square of lining fabric in
plain or solid color
Sewing thread to match
240 plastic drop beads (hole across
the top), assorted colors
1,000 one-color plastic ¼ in. round
beads
240 one-color plastic tube
½ x ¼ in. beads
Forty one-color plastic rondelle
½ in. beads
Forty one-color plastic faceted
¼ in. beads
Button sewing thread to match
the beads
Hank of contrast embroidery thread
for the edge
Roll of very fine beading wire
Round-nose pliers
Wire snippers or scissors
Sewing machine
Sewing kit

  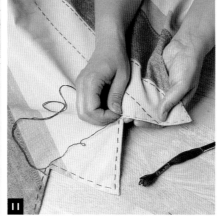 

1 With the wire snippers, cut 240 pieces of the beading wire 4 in. long to make the tassels. **2** Take one length of wire and attach a drop bead to one end. With the round-nose pliers, bend the tail end of the wire and twist it over to keep the bead from falling off. Bead on four round ¼ in. beads and one tube bead. **3** With the pliers, make a loop at the top of the tube bead (this should be at the center of the wire), and bead the remaining length of wire with one tube bead and four round ¼ in. beads. **4** Finish with a drop bead, twisted securely in place. Use different colors of drop beads for each tassel for contrast. Make up forty. **5** To make up the tablecloth, see the diagram on page 251 for a cutting guide for the corners. Each side of the cloth has nine points measuring 4¾ in. from point to point, with a ½ in. hem around the edge of the fabric. **6** Use the lining fabric for marking up the measurements with a dressmaker's pencil or chalk. First measure and mark all four corners and then measure and mark nine triangles down each side. **7** Pin or baste the main fabric with the right side out to the lining and cut both together along the marked lines. Keep the two pieces of fabric pinned or basted together until all the sewing is complete. **8** Choose one of the colors in the fabric and cut a workable length of contrast color embroidery thread. **9** Separate the thread into three strands and thread a needle. Sew a running stitch down the sides of each stripe of your chosen color. This will act to hold the two pieces of fabric together. **10** Fold and iron ½ in. hems on all the edges of both pieces, and using a matching thread, slipstitch the lining to the main cloth. Iron all edges. **11** Cut another workable length of contrast color embroidery thread and separate it into three strands. Thread a needle with the strands and sew a neat running stitch ¼ in. in from the edge of the tablecloth. Remove all the pins or basting threads and iron if necessary. **12** To attach the tassels to the points, use the button sewing thread in a color to match the beads, knot the end, and stitch the thread through one point in the cloth from back to front. Bead on one faceted ½ in. bead, then a rondelle bead, then three of the beaded strands by the loops in the middle, and draw the tassel up to the point. **13** Now bring the needle back up through the rondelle and faceted beads and stitch back through the point in the tablecloth. Pull the beads tight. Make a neat knot at the back of the fabric and cut off. Do this to all the points on the tablecloth.

stamped plant pots

These terra-cotta pots are first painted with acrylic gesso—a plaster-based paint used by artists to prime their canvases. It covers the porous surface of terra-cotta very well and is easily tinted with acrylic paints. The checkerboard pattern is stamped with gold acrylic paint.

 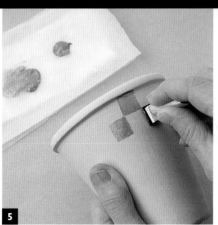 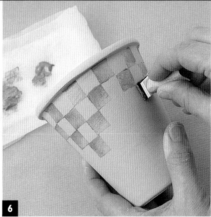 

1 Mix a small amount of colored acrylic paint with gesso to achieve a pale pastel color. Add a small quantity of black to dull the color slightly. Paint the terra-cotta pot inside and out with two coats of tinted gesso, allowing it to dry between coats. **2** Cut a square of neoprene, ½ in. for a large pot and ¼ in. for a small pot. Stick the neoprene to a square of thick cardboard and add a suitable handle such as a narrow cotton reel or coiled cardboard. **3** Make a stamping pad by sandwiching a damp folded paper towel between two layers of silicone paper. This keeps the paint from drying too quickly. **4** Drop a small amount of paint onto the silicone paper and work it into a thin layer with the stamp. Try out some prints on a spare piece of paper. You may have to roll the stamp from top to bottom and side to side to make a clean square print. **5** Print a square just under the rim of the pot, then print a square touching each bottom corner of the first row to create a checkerboard pattern. **6** Work down the pot in a V shape. Overlap the corners slightly as you go down the pot to accommodate the curved sides. This is more pronounced in larger sizes. **7** Use the same stamp to print a gold band around the rim of the pot. Roll the stamp over the rim and stop the same distance inside the pot each time. **8** When dry, apply two coats of clear varnish.

materials

Terra-cotta garden pots
Acrylic gesso
Acrylic paints in colors of black, purple, green, dark red, gold
Neoprene foam sheet
Acrylic varnish
Silicone paper
Cardboard or empty cotton reel
Thick cardboard
Paintbrush
Paper towel

templates

leaf blind
Actual size

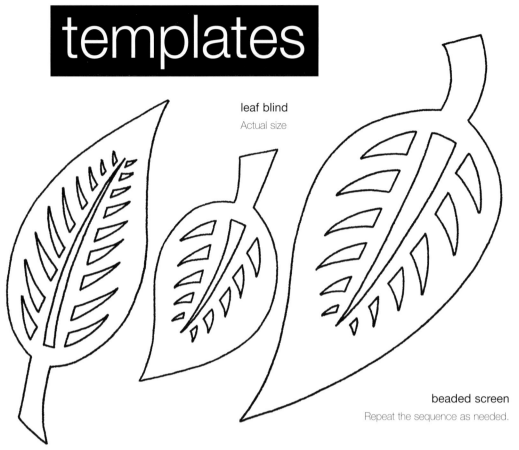

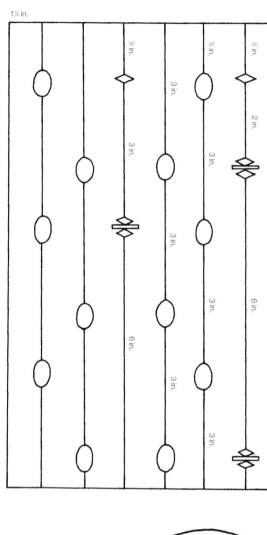

beaded screen
Repeat the sequence as needed.

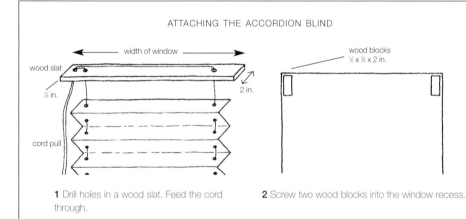

ATTACHING THE ACCORDION BLIND

width of window

wood slat

1⁄4 in.

cord pull

wood blocks
1⁄2 x 3⁄4 x 2 in.

2 in.

1 Drill holes in a wood slat. Feed the cord through.

2 Screw two wood blocks into the window recess.

1⁄4 x 2 in. MDF

cleat

3 Glue the top of the blind to the wood slat. Screw the slat onto the base of the small blocks.

4 Glue a piece of MDF to the front of the blocks with wood glue as a facing board. Secure with panel pins. Screw a cleat to the wall.

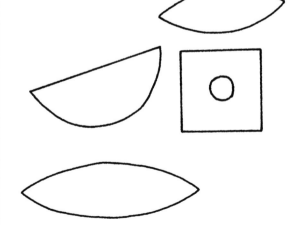

accordion blind
Actual size

red

pink

yellow

dark green

dark blue

pale blue

pale green

dark blue

pale blue

black

pale blue

purple

pale green

dark green

yellow

beaded sheer curtain

Actual size

yellow

black

dark green

pale green

dark blue

pale blue

tulip screen (1)
Increase between the markings to 10½ in.

tulip screen (2)
Increase between the markings to 6¼ in.

tulip screen (6)
Increase between the markings to 8½ in.

tulip screen (7)
Increase between the markings to 8¼ in.

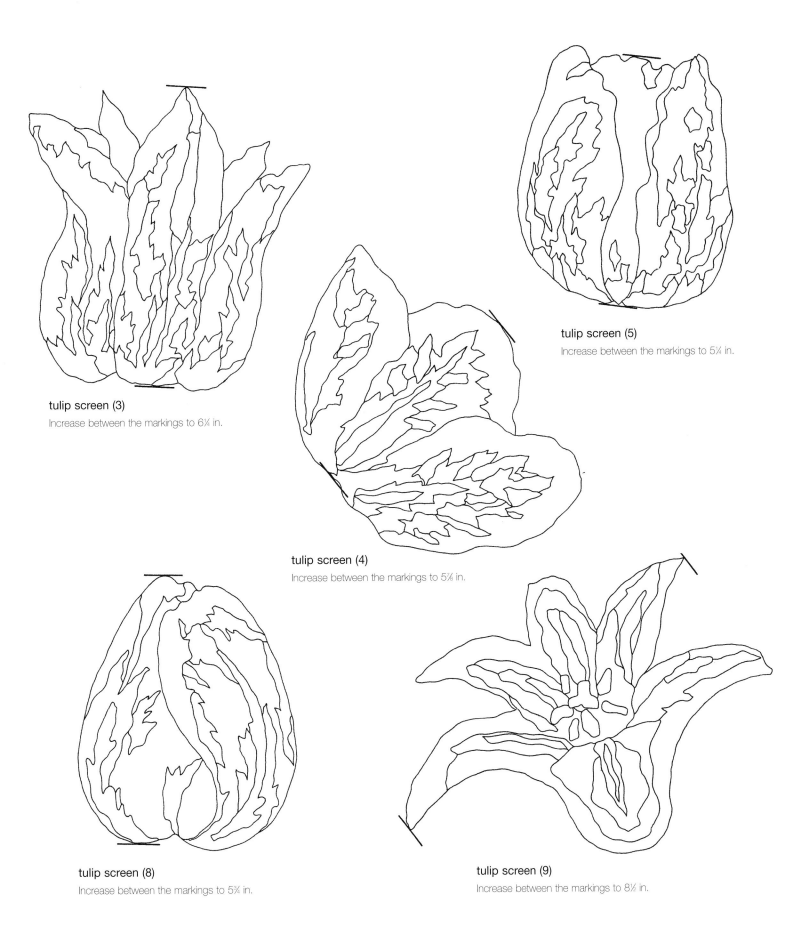

tulip screen (3)
Increase between the markings to 6¼ in.

tulip screen (4)
Increase between the markings to 5⅞ in.

tulip screen (5)
Increase between the markings to 5¼ in.

tulip screen (8)
Increase between the markings to 5¾ in.

tulip screen (9)
Increase between the markings to 8½ in.

ice poppies bed linen
Actual size

lavender bags
heart motif
Actual size

laurel leaf chest of drawers
Actual size
Reverse the image at the broken line.

lavender bags
envelope-flap bag
Actual size

plant stand
Enlarge as needed.

stamped blanket box
Actual size

mosaic tabletop
Actual size

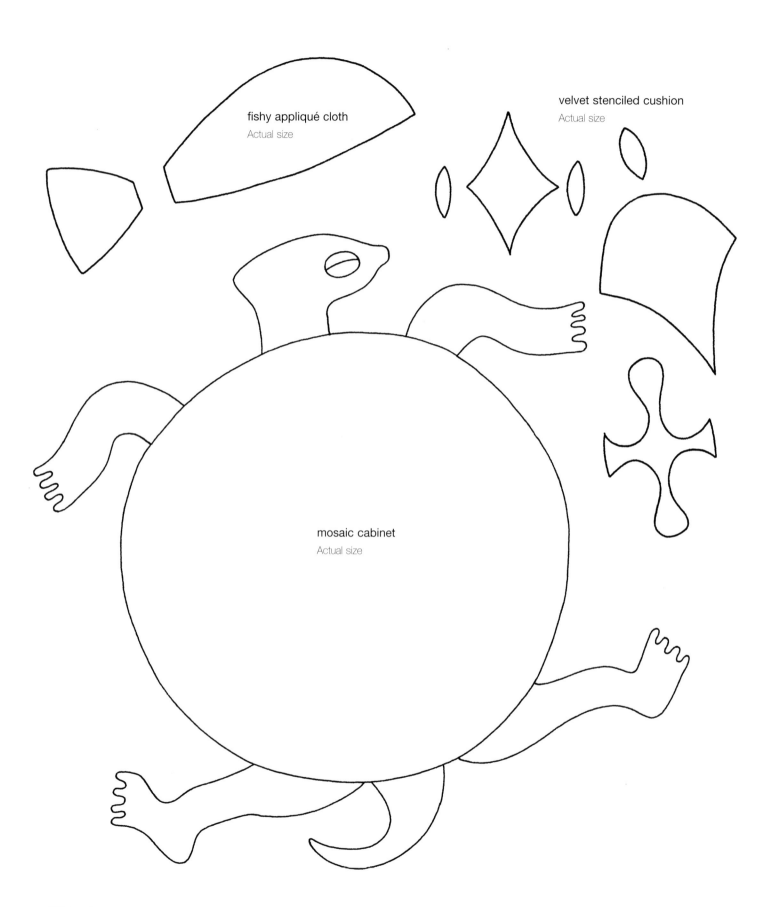

fishy appliqué cloth
Actual size

velvet stenciled cushion
Actual size

mosaic cabinet
Actual size

shoe box

Increase length to 9¾ in.

seaside tablecloth and napkins

Actual size

Stamp is defined by the blue line.

Stencil is defined by the black lines.

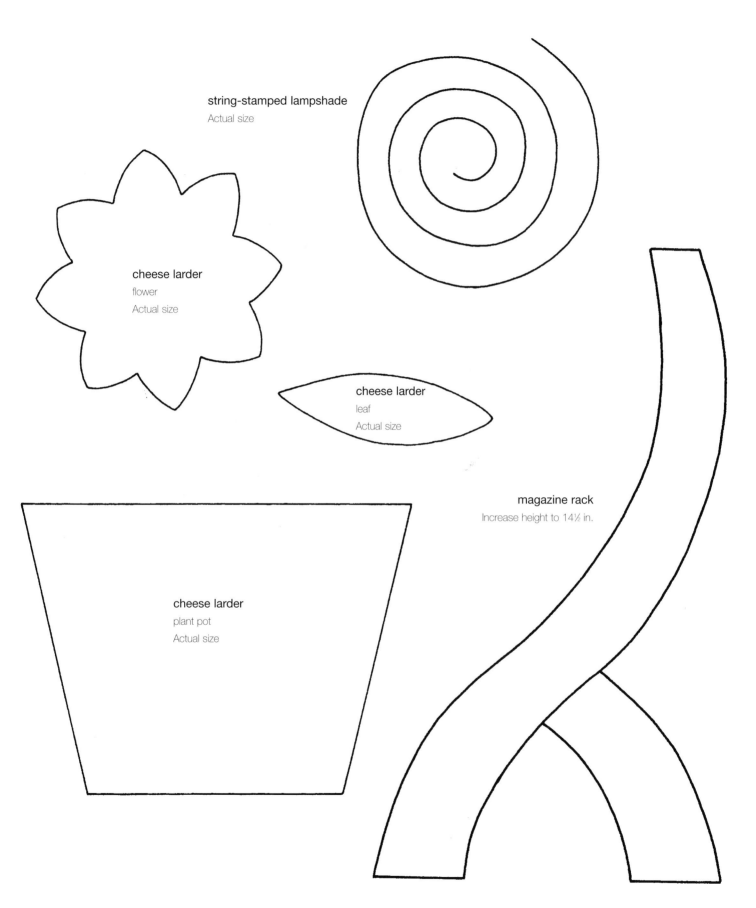

string-stamped lampshade
Actual size

cheese larder
flower
Actual size

cheese larder
leaf
Actual size

magazine rack
Increase height to 14½ in.

cheese larder
plant pot
Actual size

黒人音楽をして以来、欲求不満のなった。べ物質的な豊

Japanese lamp
Enlarge text as needed.

accordion wall light
Actual size

stained-glass vase
Enlarge as needed.

*A B C D E F G H I J K L M
N O P Q R S T U V W X Y Z*

stenciled letter holder
Enlarge as needed.

hand ring holder
Actual size

stenciled letter holder
pomegranate
Actual size

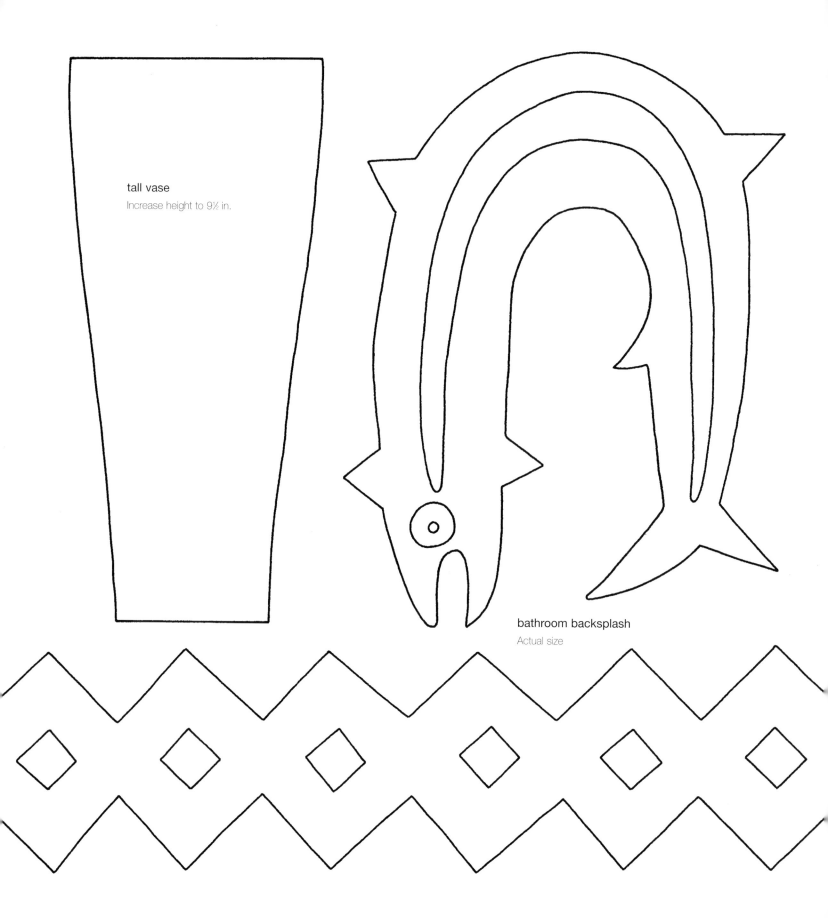

tall vase
Increase height to 9½ in.

bathroom backsplash
Actual size

blanket mats

Actual size

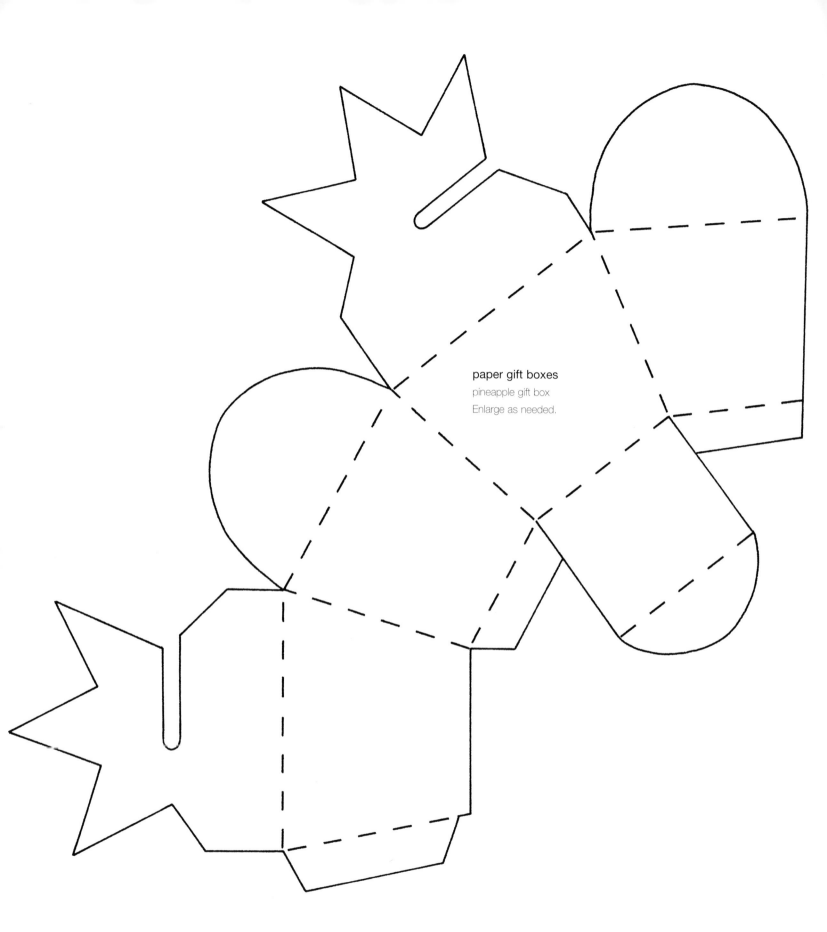

paper gift boxes
pineapple gift box
Enlarge as needed.

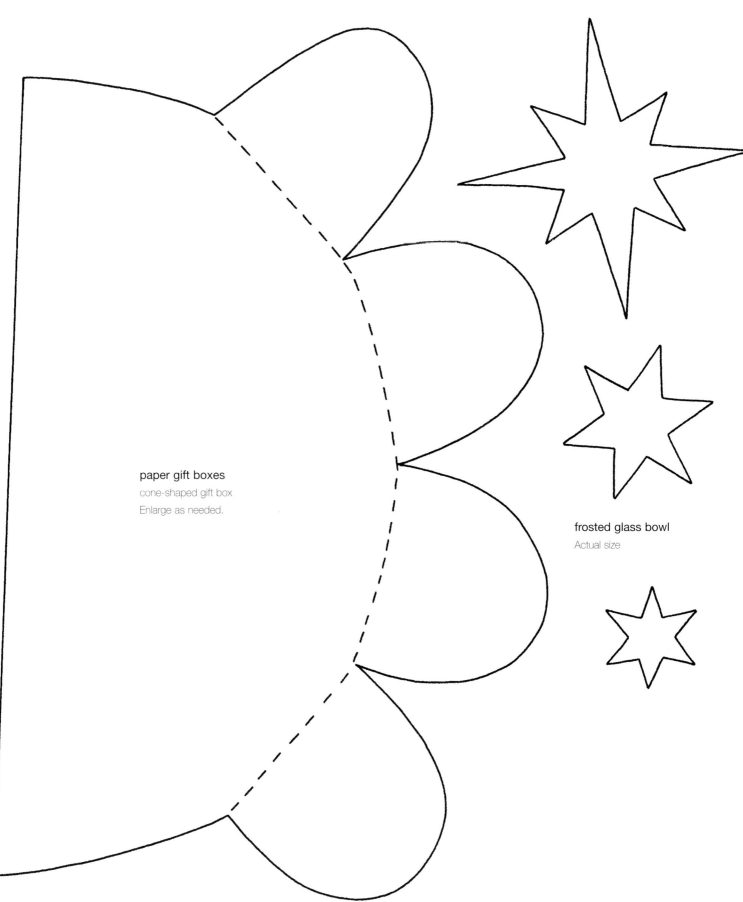

paper gift boxes

cone-shaped gift box

Enlarge as needed.

frosted glass bowl

Actual size

frosted window stencil

Enlarge to fit your windowpane.

frosted window stencil

Enlarge to fit your windowpane.

frosted window stencil

Enlarge to fit your windowpane.

cut-paper shelf edging

Half of the image is shown.

Reverse the image at the broken line.

Increase the depth between the red lines to 5¼ in.

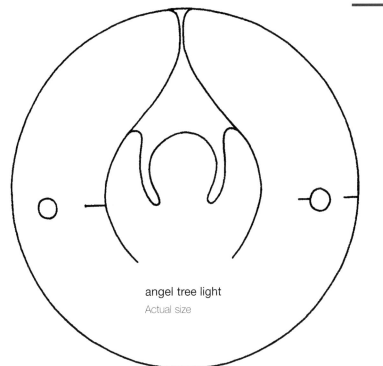

angel tree light

Actual size

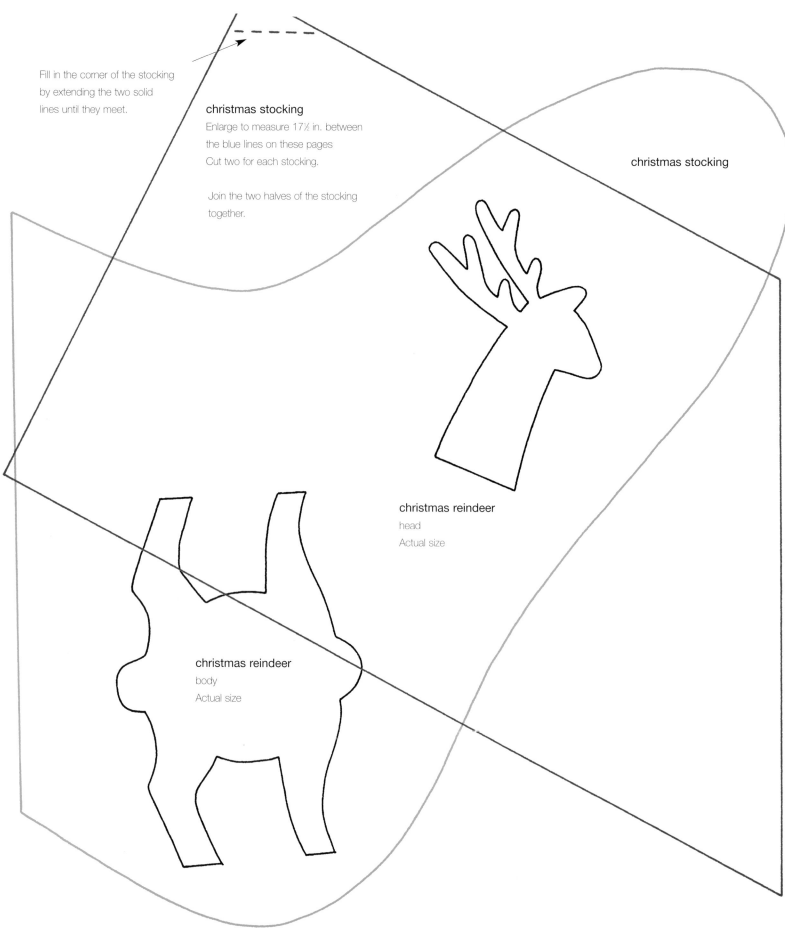

Fill in the corner of the stocking
by extending the two solid
lines until they meet.

christmas stocking

Enlarge to measure 17½ in. between
the blue lines on these pages
Cut two for each stocking.

Join the two halves of the stocking
together.

christmas stocking

christmas reindeer
head
Actual size

christmas reindeer
body
Actual size

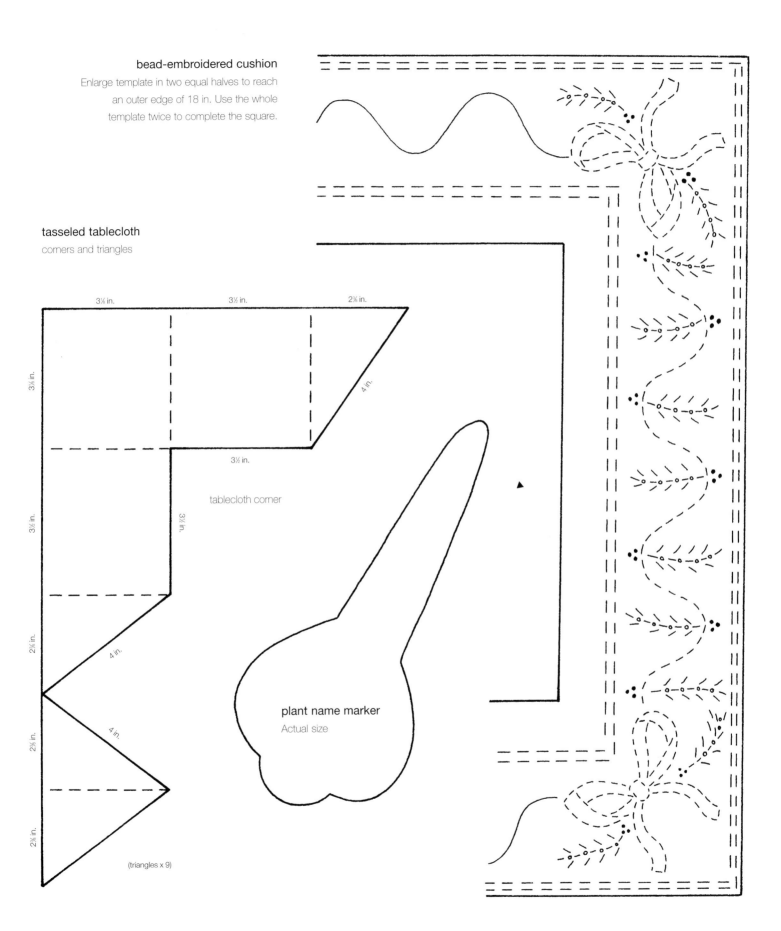

bead-embroidered cushion

Enlarge template in two equal halves to reach
an outer edge of 18 in. Use the whole
template twice to complete the square.

tasseled tablecloth

corners and triangles

3⅛ in.

3½ in.

2⅜ in.

3⅛ in.

4 in.

3½ in.

3⅜ in.

tablecloth corner

3½ in.

4 in.

2⅜ in.

plant name marker

Actual size

4 in.

2⅜ in.

2⅜ in.

(triangles x 9)

window box

Actual size

index

a

accordion blind 26–7, 230
accordion wall light 112–13, 239
aluminum mesh basket 168–9
angel tree lights 178–9, 249
appliqué 76

b

backsplash: bathroom backsplash
    150–51, 242
bags
    chenille drawstring 66–7
    lavender 58–9, 234
baskets
    aluminum mesh 168–9
    egg 98–9
    hanging flower 222–3
    rose storage 102–3
    wastebasket 84–5
bathroom backsplash 150–51, 242
bead-embroidered cushion 224–5,
    251
beaded candle holder 126–7
beaded fruit 170–71
beaded lampshade 110–11
beaded screen 22–3, 230
beaded sheer curtain 28–9, 231
beaded table runners 216–17
beaded-wire picture frame 142–3
beads 22, 23, 26, 27, 28, 31, 75, 85,
    111, 113, 127, 130, 131, 156,
    160, 161, 217, 222, 225, 226
bed linen, ice poppies 56–7, 234
blanket box, stamped 44–5, 235
blanket mats 164–5, 243
blinds
    accordion 26–7, 230
    leaf 18–19, 230
    unstructured 16–17
bowls
    frosted glass 166–7, 245
    lace paper 146–7
    salad 156–7
boxes
    paper gift 176–7, 244, 245
    shoe 92–3, 237
    stamped blanket 44–5, 235
buttoned place mats 218–19
buttoned up cushions 60–61
buttons
    mother-of-pearl 59, 60, 159
    shell 14, 218

c

cabinet, mosaic 90–91, 236
calico 16, 17, 207
candle holders, beaded 126–7
candles, garden 212–13
cane 120, 121, 122, 123
canvas 79, 203
chairs
    crackle-glazed 42–3
    director's chair loose cover 220–21
    upholstery tack 52–3
cheese larder 96–7, 238
chenille drawstring bag 66–7
chest, letter 94–5
chests of drawers
    decoupage 40–41
    laurel leaf 46–7, 234
chintz 130, 131
chocolate wreath 190–91
Christmas 172–3
    angel tree lights 178–9, 249
    chocolate wreath 190–91
    Christmas reindeer 194–5, 250
    Christmas stockings 184, 250
    cut-paper shelf edging 186–7, 249
    embossed velvet tablecloth 188–9
    folded paper pinecones 174–5
    frosted window stencil 182–3, 246,
      247, 248
    mistletoe kissing bough 196–7
    paper gift boxes 176–7, 244, 245
    ribbon and ornament curtain 180–1
    twisted wire decorations 192–3
cloth: patchwork picnic cloth 206–7
coil pots 100–101
coils, wirework 11, 100–101
cotton 20, 57, 155, 205, 207, 226
cotton duck canvas 79
crackle-glazed chairs 42–3
crackle-glazed finish 35
crochet 85, 160
cupboard, metallic effect 38–9
curtains
    beaded sheer 28–9, 231
    denim 24–5
    knitted hemp 30–31
cushions
    bead-embroidered 224–5, 251
    buttoned up 60–61
    floor 204–5
    secret color 72–3
    tied 70–71
    velvet stenciled 62–3, 236

cut-paper shelf edging 186–7, 249
cutwork 92, 93

d

decoupage
    chest 40–41
    letter chest 94–5
denim curtain 24–5
director's chair loose cover 220–21
display 124–5
    bathroom splashback 150–51, 242
    beaded candle holder 126–7
    beaded-wire picture frame 142–3
    hammered mirror frame 136–7
    hand ring holder 138–9, 241
    handmade paper notebooks 132–3
    lace paper bowls 146–7
    mini soap blocks 148–9
    paper picture frames 144–5
    photograph album 130–31
    stained-glass vase 128–9, 240
    stenciled letter holder 134–5, 240
    tall vases 140–41, 242
duvet cover: ice poppies bed linen
    56–7

e

egg basket 98–9
embossed velvet tablecloth 188–9
embroidery 68, 184, 225
entertaining 152–3
    aluminum mesh basket 168–9
    beaded fruit 170–71
    blanket mats 164–5, 243
    frosted glass bowl 166–7, 245
    raffia table runner 160–61
    round platter 162–3
    salad bowl 156–7
    serving spoons 158–9
    simple place mats 154–5

f

felt 184
fishy appliqué cloth 76–7, 236
floor cushion 204–5
floor tiles 50, 51
floorcloth, painted 78–9
flower box, lavender 208–9
folded paper pinecones 174–5
frosted glass bowl 166–7, 245
frosted window stencil 182–3, 246,
    247, 248
furniture 34–5

crackle-glazed chairs 42–3
    decoupage chest 40–41
    laurel leaf chest of drawers 46–7,
      234
    metallic effect cupboard 38–9
    mosaic tabletop 48–9, 235
    plant stand 50–51, 235
    stamped blanket box 44–5, 235
    studded coffee table 36–7
    upholstery tack chair 52–3

g

garden candles 212–13
glass jar lanterns 116–17
glorious organza 14–15

h

hammered mirror frame 136–7
hammock 202–3
hand ring holder 138–9, 241
handmade paper notebooks 132–3
hanging flower basket 222–3
hemp 31

i

ice poppies bed linen 56–7, 234

j

Japanese lamp 108–9, 239

k

knitted hemp curtain 30–31

l

lace paper bowls 146–7
lamps
    Momigami lamp 122–3
    woven cane lamp 120–21
lampshades
    beaded 110–11
    parchment 114–15
    string stamped 118–19, 238
lanterns, glass jar 116–17
lattice-work 97
laundry box 88–9
laurel leaf chest of drawers 46–7, 234
lavender bags 58–9, 234
lavender flower box 208–9
leaf blind 18–19, 230
letter chest 94–5
letter holder, stenciled 134–5, 240
lighting 106–7
    accordion wall light 112–13, 239

beaded lampshade 110–11
glass jar lanterns 116–17
Japanese lamp 108–9, 239
Momigami lamp 122–3
parchment shade 114–15
string stamped lampshade 118–19, 238
woven cane lamp 120–21
linen 16, 17, 20, 60, 64, 68, 71, 72, 76, 205, 217
linens 54–5
buttoned up cushions 60–61
chenille drawstring bag 66–7
fishy appliqué cloth 76–7
ice poppies bed linen 56–7, 234
lavender bags 58–9, 234
organdy tablecloth 74–5
ribbon embroidery throw 68–9
seaside tablecloth & napkins 64–5, 237
secret color cushion 72–3
tied cushion 70–71
velvet stenciled cushions 62–3, 236
loose cover, director's chair 220–21

m
magazine rack 82–3, 238
mats, blanket 164–5, 243
metallic effect cupboard 38–9
mini soap blocks 148–9
mirror frame, hammered 136–7
mistletoe kissing bough 196–7
Momigami lamp 122–3
mosaic
bathroom backsplash 150–51
mosaic cabinet 90–91, 236
mosaic tabletop 48–9, 235
round platter 162–3

n
napkins: seaside tablecloth & napkins 64–5, 237
neoprene sheet 26, 27, 229
notebooks, handmade paper 132–3

o
organdy 59, 75
organdy tablecloth 74–5
organza 14, 28, 76
outdoor living 198–9
beaded table runners 216–17
bead-embroidered cushion 224–5, 251
buttoned place mats 218–19
director's chair loose cover 220–21
floor cushion 204–5

garden candles 212–13
hammock 202–3
hanging flower basket 222–3
lavender flower box 208–9
parasol changing tent 200–201
patchwork picnic cloth 206–7
plant name marker 210–11, 250
stamped plant pots 228–9
tasseled tablecloth 226–7, 251
window box 214–15, 251

p
painted floorcloth 78–9
paper gift boxes 176–7, 244, 245
paper picture frames 144–5
papier-mâché 147
parasol changing tent 200–201
parchment shade 114–15
patchwork picnic cloth 206–7
photograph album 130–31
picture frames
beaded-wire 142–3
paper 144–5
pillowcase: ice poppies bed linen 56–7
place mats
buttoned 218–19
simple 154–5
plant name marker 210–11, 250
plant pots, stamped 228–9
plant stand 50–51, 235
platter, round 162–3

r
rack, twisted wire hook 104–5
raffia table runner 160–61
ribbon 68, 102, 141, 177, 181
ribbon and ornament curtain 180–81
ribbon embroidery throw 68–9
ring holder, hand 138–9, 241
rose storage basket 102–3
round platter 162–3

s
safety 10
salad bowl 156–7
screens
beaded 22–3, 230
tulip 32–3, 232
seaside tablecloth & napkins 64–5, 237
secret color cushion 72–3
sequins 171
serving spoons 158–9
sewing kit 10
shackled heading 20–21

shelf edging, cut-paper 186–7, 249
shoe boxes 92–3, 237
shoji paper 108
silk 67, 76
simple place mats 154–5
soap: mini soap blocks 148–9
spoons: serving spoons 158–9
stained-glass vase 128–9, 240
stamped blanket box 44–5, 235
stamped plant pots 228–9
stamping 10, 26, 44, 48, 53, 57, 64, 118, 188, 229
stenciled letter holder 134–5, 240
stenciling 10, 35, 39, 47, 63, 64, 79, 113, 135, 167, 183
storage 80–81
cheese larder 96–7, 238
coil pots 100–101
egg basket 98–9
laundry box 88–9
letter chest 94–5
magazine rack 82–3, 238
mosaic cabinet 90–91, 236
rose storage basket 102–3
shoe boxes 92–3, 237
storage bin 86–7
twisted wire hook rack 104–5
waste paper basket 84–5
string stamped lampshade 118–19, 238
studded coffee table 36–7
suede 130, 131

t
table runners
beaded 216–17
raffia 160–61
tablecloths
embossed velvet 188–9
fishy appliqué 76–7, 236
organdy 74–5
seaside tablecloth & napkins 64–5, 237
tasseled 226–7, 251
tables
mosaic table top 48–9, 235
studded coffee 36–7
tall vases 140–41, 242
tasseled tablecloth 226–7, 251
templates 230–51
tent, parasol changing 200–201
throw, ribbon embroidery 68–9
tied cushion 70–71
tiles 215
ceramic wall 90, 91
floor 50, 51

glass mosaic 90, 91, 163
tree lights, angel 178–9, 249
tulip screen 32–3, 232
twisted wire decorations 192–3
twisted wire hook rack 104–5

u
unstructured blind 16–17
upholstery tack chair 52–3

v
vases
stained-glass vase 128–9, 240
tall vases 140–41, 242
velvet 63, 188
chenille 67
velvet stenciled cushions 62–3, 236

w
wall light, accordion 112–13
wastebasket 84–5
window box 214–15, 251
window dressing 12–13
accordion blind 26–7, 230
beaded screen 22–3, 230
beaded sheer curtain 28–9, 231
denim curtain 24–5
glorious organza 14–15
knitted hemp curtain 30–31
leaf blind 18–19, 230
shackled heading 20–21
tulip screen 32–3, 232
unstructured blind 16–17
wirework
aluminum mesh basket 168–9
beaded candle holder 127–8
beaded lampshade 110–11
beaded-wire picture frame 142–3
chocolate wreath 190–91
coil pots 100–101
coils 11
egg basket 98–9
glass jar lanterns 116–17
hand ring holder 138–9
hanging flower basket 222–3
mistletoe kissing bough 196–7
rose storage basket 102–3
twisted wire hook rack 104–5
twisting wire 11
woven cane lamp 120–21